FROM THE TOP OF THE STAIRS

FROM THE
TOP
OF THE
STAIRS

Gretchen Finletter

An Atlantic Monthly Press Book

Little, Brown and Company · Boston

1946

To MA *and* PA

Contents

Contents

FROM THE TOP OF THE STAIRS

Hotels and Rehearsals

BEFORE I went to school, I thought — if I thought about it at all — that all fathers lunched at home and that all houses were filled with the sounds of the rehearsals of singers or wind instruments. Front halls quite naturally had a couple of cellos standing in them, dressed in neat brown overcoats which under no conditions must be touched. I thought most homes had at least three pianos.

Pianos followed us everywhere. They came up trunk elevators in hotels, they were hauled by ropes through apartment house windows, and in the country they were drawn by farm horses in great wagons. They were usually the largest grands that Steinway's could furnish. It never seemed possible when they were delivered, with the legs off and their strings exposed, that they could be fitted together, and my sisters and I would watch anxiously to see if they would really turn into complete instruments again. The men apparently knew what they were about, but the grands always looked ruined.

Finally my father would sit down and strike some great chords.

"Well, Mr. Damrosch, how do you like her?" he was asked expectantly.

"Beautiful tone. Boys, tell Mr. Steinway that is the finest piano I have had yet."

He continued to play, and it always seemed to me that the improvisations to try out the new piano were a little lovelier, a little more noble, than the music of ordinary days. The men would stand about listening, and suddenly my father would spring up and give them each a cigar, while one of them would tell him the latest story of what had happened to some artist on tour when his piano in the baggage car had gone on the wrong siding.

Performances became a reality to me when I was very small. We were spending the winter at the Cambridge Hotel, a small hotel on Fifth Avenue across from the old Waldorf. My father was conducting at the Metropolitan Opera House. To live in a hotel was deeply exciting to my sisters and me. Polly was a very little girl and shared a room with our nurse Minnie, and Alice and I had a room together.

The room had folding beds. In the daytime they looked like two tall highboys with small desks fitted into the sides, but at night they unhooked, the desks mysteriously disappeared, and the highboys became beds. Alice, who was three years older than I and much bolder, immediately learned the trick and would rush in in the evening and fold them up again to see if our little desks were still there and why the ink did not spill. She would never let me see how she did it — it was her secret — but she often hinted that if I did not do what she wanted she might fold me up at night. This made going to bed an adventure, because I was never sure if I, or a completely flattened I, would be there in the morning.

Children love hotels. In the first place, the food is so interesting. Try as a mother or nurse will to reproduce the wholesomeness of home, a waiter desiring to be popular will always sneak in some gay novelty of his own. We had an Italian waiter called Roberto, and we found him both handsome and resourceful. He began by teaching us how to fold napkins in the beautiful way he did, to resemble cabbages or swans. Then he rolled the butter like a setting hen, with the butter ball as eggs. With the aid of the chef, who liked opera and admired my father, he brought us pastries iced very brightly to resemble the flags of the nations. We were told the blue icing was poison and to eat very carefully around it.

The Cambridge had long red-carpeted halls. If one slid one's feet along them, one could give electric shocks to the people one touched. There came up through the shafts a permanent and delicious smell of hot bread. My mother and father did not enjoy this smell, but to us it seemed that the hotel was perpetually getting ready for a party.

New guests came and went, and it was interesting to watch them, study the labels on their luggage, and see if there might be other children. Roberto had very sharply defined opinions of the newcomers and he confided in us as if we were old stand-bys. It was flattering to be treated as his understanding equals, and at breakfast he would tell us who had come and what significant clues there were to their characters.

We shook our heads sympathetically with him as he told us of the first dinner given the night before by a new arrival: "There are five of them and he orders the dinner. Then I show him the wine card. He orders *one* bottle — one bottle for five! I fool him. I open another bottle. I shame him into behaving like a gentleman!"

"Good for you, Roberto," we congratulated.

Thus there became fixed in my mind forever the conviction that no gentleman ever tries to serve five people from one bottle. I was six years old.

Minnie, our nurse, never quite knew how to treat Roberto. She was Swedish and had a natural contempt for Latins. She also loved horror stories. She did not encourage Roberto and she wore a haughty look while he talked, but sometimes she lingered after we had left the dining room, to hear some further details of the new guests that Roberto seemed to think we should be spared. Then she would ejaculate to herself in the elevator, "Akeekock!" All her life, this was her expression for anything that disgusted her, and it was used equally for the sins of the flesh and the carelessness of a child who did not wear her rubbers.

The event of the week was the day when a performance was given. My father seemed to change completely. He would appear in a full-dress suit while the sun was still shining through the windows, and instead of eating a real dinner downstairs, he would take some tea and toast in our little sitting room while he looked frequently at his watch. Then with a pale face he would go off in the twilight in his high silk hat, carrying the score under his arm.

The next event was to hook my mother up. First she put on a beautiful satin evening dress while Minnie stood by as official hooker-upper. There seemed to be hundreds of hooks, and if they went first from right to left, they recrossed from left to right with tinier eyes. Even if little Polly called from her room, nothing could interrupt this moment. We would stand about, urging my mother to wear this pin or that necklace, and spreading our suggestions in alluring combinations.

Next my mother would take from the glove box a long pair of French kid gloves. They had eight little buttons which had to be buttoned with a special glove hook. Finally she put on a wonderful evening wrap which one of us had been trying on in front of the mirror; then she too went out into the evening, took a cab, and drove to the opera.

Minnie carefully locked up the jewel box, and the rooms became silent. Alice and I went to our folding beds and to sleep. But we were wakened several hours later by a roar of noise. The performance was over and late supper was in progress. There were guests and there floated in to us the sound of clinking glasses. Everyone was gay and relaxed, and my father's voice sounded louder and happier than anyone else's.

"Where is the champagne?" Pop went a cork. "Let us drink to Lillian Nordica. To the finest performance of Elsa that I believe has ever been heard!"

Applause, the scrape of chairs, and the voice of Madame Nordica: "Thank you, my dear, dear friends. And now, Walter, let me drink to you."

But I was anxiously doing some arithmetic. There were eight people, and so far only one cork had popped. Bing, a second one. Good. Was two for eight better than one for five? Bang, and a third bottle was opened. I lay back greatly relieved, and relaxed. I must tell Roberto at breakfast. Nothing wrong with my father!

It was decided that I should attend a performance of *Siegfried*. I had never been to the opera and I had a confused idea of what it was. Staying at the Cambridge was Madame Johanna Gadski, who was singing many of the Wagnerian roles. Her daughter Lotte was a friend of Alice's. Lotte, who could not have been more than eleven years old, was general costume mistress for her mother. She was very quick with her needle and could tell at a glance what spangle or ornament was missing. She adored her mother, and at every performance was waiting in the dressing room with her faithful little thimble on her finger.

One afternoon she invited us up to have hot chocolate in their apartment. First she showed us all her mother's evening dresses. Then the costumes that were home for adjustments. Flattered by our delight, she placed Brünnhilde's helmet on Alice's head and hung

Elizabeth's necklace from *Tannhäuser* about my neck. We were dazzled. But when it came time to leave I found I had to give back the necklace. I had thought it was a real party and that the necklace was a present for keeps. I felt so badly that when we went downstairs I could not even give the elevator man a surprise electric shock.

Many of the singers had special rehearsals with my father in our sitting room. Minnie liked the Rhine Maidens and always left the door open so that we could hear them. One day when Polly and I came back from Gramercy Park with her, we saw eight very large ladies gathered about my father at the piano.

Minnie gave a snort. "They have come!"

"Who are they?" I asked.

"Wait," answered Minnie in a voice of foreboding. "You'll hear it."

"Are they bad?"

"You'll see."

The piano crashed and eight Valkyries let out a wild Hoyo-to-ho.

Minnie gave a great groan. "How is Polly going to get her nap with that going on? Akee-kock!"

But Polly gave a wide and happy smile. This was like nothing she had ever heard before. My father joined his voice with the Valkyries'. Alternately he was Wotan and Brünnhilde. The Valkyries sang in twos, in fours, in sevens. Then, when we were afraid it was finished, they began all over again, and again and again. Minnie retired into the farthest bathroom. What the rest of the hotel and the Waldorf felt, no one cared.

The next day it was raining hard. My father told my mother at lunch that he was worried about the bird.

"She is too prosaic. She doesn't give it color. I'm going over it with her upstairs at three."

"Couldn't you rehearse her at the Opera House?" begged my mother.

"No, she's frightened in front of the company. I must encourage her."

I waited around the sitting room. I wanted to see this bird and why it was so frightened.

A very stout little lady appeared, hung up a dripping raincoat, took off her hat, and stood beside the piano. My father sat down and began to play perhaps the most beautiful part of *Siegfried*, the sounds of the forest. Then he sang softly: —

> *Noch einmal, liebes Vöglein,*
> *da wir so lang' lästig gestört,*
> *lauscht' ich gerne deinem Sange. . . .*

The door was opened into Polly's room and we all listened. The bird now answered in a silvery voice: —

Hei! Siegfried erschlug nun den schlimmen Zwerg!
Jetzt wüsst' ich ihm noch das herrlichste Weib —

"No, no!" cried my father. "You are not announcing that dinner is served. You are bringing glorious tidings to Siegfried! For God's sake, be joyous!"

The bird gave an apologetic smile.

"One, two," said my father, conducting with his right hand.

> *Auf hohem Felsen sie schläft,*
> *Feuer umbrennt ihren Saal —*

"You're high up in the air!" exclaimed my father. "Fräulein Schnee, I beg you, don't be so pedestrian!"

The bird now looked stubborn. The heavenly music began again.

> *Durchschritt' er die Brunst,*
> *weckt er die Braut,*
> *Brünnhilde wäre dann sein!*

We listened, agonizing for the bird. She sang and my father sang with her, making two birds. They continued together.

> *Lustig im Leid sing' ich von Liebe.*

"One, two," said my father. The bird jumped in alone.

> *Wonnig und Weh' web' ich mein Lied:*
> *nur Sehnende kennen den Sinn!*

"Watch my beat!"

My mother appeared in the hall and hissed at me.

"Tell your father I have gone for a long, long walk!"

"Again!" ordered my father, and they sang together.

> *Die Braut gewinnt,*
> *Brünnhild' erweckt*
> *ein Feiger nie —*

Then the bird burst into tears.

"My dear child," screamed my father, "I am only trying to give you *confidence!*"

> *nur wer das Fürchten nicht kennt!*

It was over. They shook hands and we helped her on with her raincoat. I told my father that my mother had gone for a long, long walk.

"In this weather?" said my father, surprised. "Why?"

It was a great question with me what I should wear to *Siegfried*. Alice and I each had Roman sashes of beautiful striped silk with long fringes, which my father had brought us from Italy. We wore them on white dresses and they were so heavy that the bows behind looked like big bustles. But I had another sash that I wanted to wear. Whenever my father received a wreath or basket of flowers to celebrate some occasion, there was always attached to it a great satin ribbon with gold lettering.

These were given to us, and we cut them up for sashes. Polly and I had equally divided the last trophy. It happened to be purple, and across my stomach was printed in gold letters, "To Commemorate Beet," while around Polly's waist appeared, "hoven's Ninth Symphony." In the end I agreed to wear the Roman sash.

Minnie took us to the Metropolitan. She wore a white silk blouse with yellow embroidery, and this was to be her best blouse for many, many years. She brought with her her opera glasses, which my mother had given her and which remained in her possession unbroken for the rest of her life. She allowed me to look through them, and of course I preferred peering into the large end to see how small everyone looked. I examined the people in the box next to us. I made Alice stare with me at the lady who was sitting only two feet away. Why, she was tiny! Didn't she look funny! The glasses were taken away from me.

The lights were lowered, the orchestra stopped tuning, there was applause, and suddenly my father appeared. It was too much for me. He must be made to realize I was there too. I stood up.

"Parp! Here I am!" I screamed as loud as I could.

A hand snatched me to the back of the box. A little later, feeling deeply humiliated, I was allowed to move to the front again and was once more given the opera glasses. This time I looked through the small end and studied my father. I was horrified. He was making such terrible faces, first at the orchestra and then at the singers. He would point his stick at one of them and give a frightful scowl. How could they perform? He never seemed to let them alone, but was always menacing them. I could not look at him. I turned to watch Mime scramble an egg.

The story of *Siegfried* had been told to me, but as part of the *Ring*. It is a complicated tale, and as I watched I was not sure which story I was seeing. Where were the gold in the river and my friends, the Rhine Maidens? What had happened to the Valkyries? I started to question Alice in a penetrating whisper. There were loud "shush-shs" from the neighboring boxes.

Suddenly I felt on familiar ground. Siegfried lay under a tree with bits of sunlight sifting through the leaves. Then began the soft and yearning sounds of the forest — the Waldweben. And I was in a panic. I knew the bird was coming. Already I had learned that opera is not a fairy tale: it is a professional performance, and I was aware, at the age of six, of the anxiety and nerves that go into a production. Siegfried was not just a hero: he was a singer with one eye on my father's beat. I believed the story as I saw it, I was relieved and happy when the sword was welded, but I knew that there was a great deal more to opera than just the story. The bird was coming, and she and my father had had words.

Then to my surprise she did not come. A queer little bunch of feathers was pulled across the stage, wobbling on a wire — and I could see the wire! I was triumphant and pointed it out loudly and delightedly to everyone who was sitting within five boxes. I did not hear the singing. I wanted everyone to know that I saw that wire, and with my naked eye. Again I was pulled to the back of the box.

Lotte appeared in the next intermission to take Alice to see her mother in her dressing room. I was not invited, but I did not mind until Alice returned. She had on her head Isolde's crown, which Madame Gadski had lent her until the end of the performance. There she sat, with a silver crown on her head. I hardly looked at the fire burning around Brünnhilde. I only watched Alice's head. I wanted so terribly to have a crown too.

2

Parents and Parades

PARENTS, I suppose, were as much a problem formerly as they are today. Unless one watched them like foxes, they might try out some bright new scheme of their own. Samuel Butler says in *The Way of All Flesh*: "Why cannot we be buried as eggs in neat little cells with thousand pound Bank of England notes wrapped round us and wake to find papa and mamma have been eaten by sparrows some weeks before we began to live consciously?"

I did not wish for anything so drastic. I admired my mother and father deeply, but of course I wanted them to be exactly like other parents. As I think back, no two were like another two, but there was a kind of type — a father who went downtown in the morning and didn't hang around the house, a gentle mother with marcelled hair who didn't say much.

Now here was something strange: I did not suffer for

my friends in similar predicaments. I remember one father who always kissed his little daughter's companions good-bye and gave off a great whiff of old brandy. That did not seem odd to me. I simply thought how expensive he smelled.

My first embarrassment started over my father. We had moved to a brownstone house on Madison Avenue and I had recovered from scarlet fever. To celebrate these events my mother told me I could give a party, and what was more, a party the way I wanted it. I knew exactly the way I wanted it — as near a duplication as possible of the other parties I had attended.

I had been to a big school for a year, so I only had fourteen best friends. These would have to be invited. Then my mother suggested I include a child of a friend of hers. I refused. She didn't go to my school; *ipso facto*, no one would like her.

I went out with Minnie to a stationery shop and bought a box of invitations. On each letterhead was a pale-blue shepherdess with a crook, and under her was printed: "Won't you come to my party on —— " Then there were spaces to indicate the day, the time, and the place, and in the left-hand corner was written, "The Favor of a Reply is requested."

I next demanded that my little sisters should not be around and butt in, as I hospitably put it. I particularly did not want Anita, the new little sister. She still used a bib at table and needed it. Minnie, who always liked the newest youngest the best, was very hurt by this. She was under the delusion that she could make Anita's hair curl. Her efforts only produced three corkscrews on one side. I told her that I thought Baby Anita was repulsive and I did not want my friends to see her. My mother announced that Anita was her most beautiful child.

Polly was allowed to be present by the simple expedient of telling me she did not want to come and would rather stay upstairs. This psychology always worked with me, and I begged her to attend. Though Alice seemed bossy to me, I needed her. As she was a little older, I felt she would give the whole affair tone. She was going to run the games.

It took me several days to decide what we were going to eat. Finally and with justifiable pride I brought my mother the bill of fare: creamed chicken, peas; ice cream (not the green kind); cocoa. My mother, in an imaginative burst, added snappers for the table, and peppermints.

The party was scheduled to run from four to six, with supper at half past five. At three o'clock I was waiting fully dressed, and at a quarter to four everyone had arrived.

After a nervous interval while we shook hands and eyed each other's clothes, Alice announced that the games were to start. It was a salmagundi affair with four tables at which different competitions took place: threading needles, jackstraws, Hearts, and Old Maid. The winner at each table, after pasting a gold star on a piece of red cardboard, advanced to the next event, and she who made the four stars first, won. The room became noisy and I relaxed.

But somehow the time element had been miscalculated. At ten minutes to five the games were all over and there were still forty minutes until supper. I have since seen this situation at parties for grownups, when things do not proceed according to plan, and I have recognized the panic on the face of the hostess. Alice, however, was equal to it. She merely stated that there would be a short interval before the next event.

Having taken a big dose of Sir Walter Scott, she then announced a new game called The Garde Joyeux and The Garde Douloureux. It was a kind of glorified Prisoner's Base, each side receiving high-sounding titles which they lost if they were captured.

In the middle of this my father entered the room, and at the same moment the waitress announced supper. My father then did a horrifying thing. He went to the piano and started to play a march. I was so appalled at this break with custom that I could not speak. Then I signaled to him to stop.

"Louder?" said my father and played on.

"Supper is served," repeated the waitress.

I reached the piano. "Don't play!" I begged. "None of the fathers play piano!"

"More fools they," replied my father, continuing. "Now all of you march around the room twice." We marched around the room twice and I did not dare lift my eyes.

Then something strange happened: my friends did not want to go in to supper. They wanted him to play to them again. They *liked* it. My mortification almost turned to pride, but not quite. I was not yet sure. This might only be a display of their impeccable manners. But when they shook hands with my mother and said, "Thank-you-for-the-lovely-party," it did sound almost genuine.

My mother had — and still has — strong opinions on the questions of the day. Though I never thought of it as quarreling, as children we were used to plenty of disagreement between my parents. My mother had great wit, and if she could not win by argument, she could often snatch victory by the flash of her repartee.

She was very clear and articulate and usually had the

facts at her finger tips; but if she was cornered and no retort came to her, she would announce that she had reached her conclusion because she "felt it in her bones." My father would declare he had just as many bones, they were just as sensitive, and they told him differently. But we believed my mother had some super-perceptive fluid tucked away in her anatomy.

The arguments usually took place at table and ranged all the way from William Howard Taft to how low a picture should be hung. My sisters and I would join in, defending the parent we felt was the weaker at the moment.

There were certain rules. My mother was the daughter of James G. Blaine, the great Republican leader. She therefore had a corner on political questions — and on the whole won in this field. My father went undisputed in the realm of music. But there was a great No Man's Land between those two areas. In the fought-over territory were interior decoration, religion, food, education, relatives — well, all the things that go to make up living.

I was so used to disagreement that when I began visiting my friends, I kept waiting for the scrap to start. At first the quiet meals seemed wonderful and like a beautiful set in a play, but then I would become home-sick and want to get back to where everyone cared passionately about everyone else's opinions and all expressed themselves in an unvarnished way.

The question of religion was a curving line between my parents. My father usually had a concert on Sundays and did not go to church. He did not think much of the music that was played there — I think it made him nervous — and anyhow, Sunday was his busy day. He did not, however, feel any the less religious or any less an authority with my mother in understanding the workings of the Deity. He always referred to God as The Almighty, and this practice annoyed my mother. I think she felt that if my father did not work enough at religion to go to church, as she did, and did not read the religious books, as she did, he should not be so know-it-all about what The Almighty was up to. She would tell him he didn't know what he was talking about.

My mother not only went to church but she listened carefully, and this habit sometimes caused her daughters suffering.

A new young clergyman would start in with his sermon and all would be well if he kept it on a vague and spiritual height. But if he was a practical cleric he would try to hitch his text to some question of the day and he would not always be on the party line. He might also be in a wonderful haze as to his facts.

I would receive a slight nudge from one of my sisters. But I did not need the nudge. I had heard the clergyman announce, "The Congress of the United States must make Covenants betwixt the nations, even as the Lord commanded Moses with the Tribes of Israel."

I saw my mother's face flush. Then, though I was in a sitting position, I would close my eyes and start to pray in real earnest. I would implore God to get that cleric to recant before it was too late. I knew He could do nothing with my mother.

After the Benediction the clergyman would stand outside to greet the congregation as they left the church. We always hung back far behind my mother. The clergyman would extend his hand with a peaceful smile.

"Do you not realize," my mother would demand, "that a treaty with a foreign power must be ratified by a two-thirds vote in the Senate, unlike a bill, which needs a majority in both Houses? It has nothing whatsoever to do with the Laws of Moses!"

The Reverend reeled. Here was living proof that someone had listened to him. He had been hit on the head and yet he was fascinated. Might he call? Might he bring a small quotation from a little book? It had great bearing on this very interesting question. My mother, still shaking her head disapprovingly, told him that he might come, and with red faces we walked home.

The Reverend came with his little book, but then my mother gave him three large books and told him to read them *carefully*. And then he came often and became charmed by my nonchurchgoing father. He would drop in for lunch and my father would tell him what Saint Peter said to the two Irishmen who wanted to get into Heaven, or expound his views, and the clergyman would nod in solemn agreement.

This would infuriate my mother. She had netted this bird and he was her prey. He should be able to see through my father and recognize that he had no idea what he was talking about!

My mother became a suffragist. The suffragettes in England were having a real fight, chaining themselves to posts, destroying the golf greens of members of Parliament, being jailed and then starving themselves. They were a courageous lot and broke the ground for their American sisters.

In this country there was strong feeling but it did not take so physical a form. There was a big section in the press which made fun of the women, and there were plenty of men and other women who were against the giving of the ballot. It took guts to fight for the cause, and a tough spirit to withstand the ridicule.

Alice Duer Miller ran a page in the *New York Tribune* called "Are Women People?" It was full of wit and became one of the pivotal points of the fight.

A group of women went down to Washington to attend the suffrage hearings. Chairman Webb cried out to the suffragists when they appeared: "Why do you come here and bother us!"

Alice Duer Miller answered in her column: —

> Girls, girls, the worst has happened;
> Our Cause is at its ebb,
> How could you go and do it!
> You've bothered Mr. Webb!

Concerning a Congressional obstructionist, she wrote: —

> "Oh, no, I don't approve of giving women the vote,
> Women," he said, "are something divine, apart,
> Something mysterious, precious, fair and remote,
> Caring for nothing but love, religion and art."
>
> "But women are really not like that," said I.
> "I like to think of them so," was his reply.

One of the arguments related to the prejudice that existed against women in the fields of medicine and law, and even in the church. If they went to universities and did as well as the men, why should they not have an equal chance in the professions?

I remember that then I became depressed. I was not very old and it seemed to me that if I ever got through school, which was already becoming difficult, I should not then be happily quit of it all, but should have to go on and on. In school we were told ambiguously that we must lead useful lives, but in the suffrage world words were not minced; we were told we had to have careers, and fight to hold them, and do even better than the men.

Like most little girls, I liked to play House. I did not think of having a husband, but I did think of having children — five of them, two boys and three girls. I knew their names and how old they were going to be. They were apparently going to spring full-armed like Minerva, one at the age of five, twins at age eight, one at nine, and one at nine and a half. I knew exactly how I would dress them. Now all this was to be denied me.

Did I really want to be a great lawyer? Should I be happy removing an appendix? I began to feel guilty and troubled. I studied the pictures of the London women in the Sunday papers. One was being carried off by two policemen, and another was lying on a cot swallowing an enormous hose. These women were doing this so that I could become a U.S. Senator. I ought to be grateful. I wasn't.

I wished my mother didn't care so. A lot of the other ladies seemed so unaware, and though I felt they had none of my mother's spirit, their children seemed less weighed down by their future responsibilities.

My mother planned to march in the first big suffrage parade. Nowadays women will march anywhere at the drop of a hat, dressed as drum majors or Puritan maids, but the first suffrage parade caused a lot of ridicule, and it took belief and nerve to march. My father was very proud of my mother. I think he would have paraded too if he had been invited, and he wanted her to get her due.

The parade took place on a May day, at five in the afternoon. The line of march was scheduled to go from Washington Square to Carnegie Hall, where a mass meeting was to take place in the evening.

The day before, there were notices in the papers from Mrs. Blatch giving the marchers their orders, advising them to look neat and keep their heads up, for on them depended the implications of the day.

My mother wore a white serge suit which just cleared the ground, and a white hat on the front of which was a feathered owl's head with big yellow glass eyes. The hat was held on by two long hatpins. Most of the women wore white; those who did not have this costume were in dark blue. There was also a special suffrage hat which cost thirty-nine cents, and a number of the ladies pinned it on.

The marchers were told to go in groups by profession or college. "If you have no profession or diploma," read the order, "if you are just married women, you are to march with your district to educate your Senator."

It was a perfect spring day. The crowd collected early along the line of march, and by three o'clock the sidewalks along Fifth Avenue were jammed. My mother went off to join her district, and there was a light in her eye. We each shook her by the hand and wished her luck. Then my father and his daughters struggled over to the Avenue to the Bryce house where we were to watch the great event.

We shoved our way up the crowded steps. There were hundreds of people about, and they were obviously out for the fun. They were going to make the ladies the butts for all possible humor. Passing in and out among them were the antisuffragists, distributing leaflets and wearing holy yet triumphant smiles. This march, they had little doubt, was going to fix their rivals.

We all became nervous. Suppose someone threw an egg at my mother. What ought we to do? We opened the big windows wide and looked anxiously down the empty Avenue and at the seething crowd. A fight between two women was taking place on a side street. One of them had kicked a basket of antisuffrage literature into the gutter, and a pleased circle formed. But there was an interruption. There was the sound of a distant band. All eyes turned from the two women.

Coming up the Avenue was a line of mounted police. The band sounded louder and there appeared fifty-four horsewomen of the Suffrage Cavalry, mounted on the shiniest of steeds and all wearing black hats cockaded in green and purple. On a rearing bay sat Inez Milholland in a linen crash suit. The crowd looked at that beautiful girl on her plunging animal and gasped. The parade was on.

The band drummed by and then came the marchers in straight rows, some carrying banners or slogans, and all wearing ribbons across their chests, and the suffrage emblem. Some were older women, some were young and lovely, but every face had on it an expression so resolute and serious that it silenced the milling crowd. There was a hush and then the applause began. I remember a shiver going up my spine and I was suddenly proud that I was related to this march.

Said the violently antisuffragist *New York Times:* —

It was a crowd far larger than that which greeted the homecoming of Theodore Roosevelt. Gallantry aside, one is forced to say that the paraders were well worth looking at. Many were young and attractive, nearly all were becomingly gowned, all stepped out like women unafraid.

But in its editorial the *Times* became more severe: —

If the women try hard enough to get the ballot, they will get it and play havoc with it for themselves and society if the men are not firm and wise enough, and it may well be said, masculine enough to prevent them.

There were in all some ten thousand marchers. Following the first groups came the college women in their caps and gowns, then the teachers. They received rousing cheers from their pupils, who had collected in knots and were waiting for them. A flock of high school girls swung into the line in gym suits, middy blouses, and red ties, with their arms extended to hold a great flag carried flat. "All this," said their banner, "is a Natural Consequence of Teaching Girls to Read."

Next appeared a band playing "Tramp, Tramp, Tramp, the Boys Are Marching." Those on the sidelines took up the refrain and sang, "The Girls Are Marching." Two carriages appeared, driven of course by women, in which sat white-haired suffrage veterans. Another band swept up the Avenue.

But the crowd, which was gay and excited, still wanted some fun. The parade was full of color and music; they were learning a lot of facts from the slogans;

they had never realized before that women worked in such a variety of fields; they had seen hundreds of pretty faces, which had surprised them, but they hadn't yet had a big laugh. Then the moment came.

Up the Avenue paraded the Men's League for Women Voters, eight hundred of them. There had been no attempt at uniformity in their dress. Some wore frock coats and high silk hats, some business suits and derbies. All carried little flags. Never were early Christians received with more delight by the lions. There was a roar of expectant pleasure.

As is the way of parades, traffic had to cross the Avenue and the gallant Eight Hundred were forced to pause several minutes. The sidewalks let them have it.

"Can't you fellows get a wife? Why not try up ahead!"

"Three cheers for the henpecked!"

"Where are your aprons?"

"Aw, Susie, are the dishes washed?"

"Who's minding the babies?"

The men took it good-naturedly. A distinguished doctor with a full beard stood at the head of a battalion of physicians. "Look at the bearded lady!" This sally received appreciative guffaws.

Finally the band struck up "I Want a Girl Just Like the Girl Who Married Dear Old Dad," and the brave men marched on, but there was a last, parting shot: "It's your chests you throw out, not your stomachs!"

Harvard and Princeton had sent delegations. The Harvard students wore their black gowns and mortarboards. When they passed the Union Club they waved at the members who were sitting in the windows. They were met by stony looks of disapproval. In this instance the sex was not hanging together.

We were still at the Bryce windows waiting for my mother. The parade continued, more bands — there were twenty-six of them — more women, a group of actresses, the laundry workers, the milliners, more districts. Then one of my sisters screamed out: "Look — in the second line — at the end!"

There was a white hat with an owl's head in front. My father stood up. "Now, when I give the signal."

The line drew nearer. "One, two, three," cried my father. "Hip, hip, hooray, hooray, hooray!"

We all cheered. The crowd joined in and cheered with us. We waved our handkerchiefs. But my mother kept her eyes straight ahead. She says she never heard us.

3

The Always Ready Club

ONE day at Miss Spence's School, a teacher announced a plan which she said must last us our lifetime and through all the trials and ordeals that would come to us. The teacher was Miss Bovee, who taught a subject known as Elocution. Her demand was that even if her pupils were faced by a major operation, a war, or a proposal of marriage — much giggling from the little girls — they must be able, as members of Miss Bovee's Always Ready Club, should the surgeon, general, or lover cry "Recite!" to give immediately three poems without a single mistake, and *with expression*.

Miss Bovee was completely successful. I do not believe that I or any of the other girls in her classes have ever forgotten our three recitations, and under strange circumstances they rise to our lips, with expression.

The school of some three hundred girls had Elocution once a week, in classes of eight, for forty-five minutes. We were required to learn a minimum of sixteen lines a week and our range of selection was extremely limited. The schooner *Hesperus* was sunk some eighty times a term, a hundred more reciters brought the good news from Ghent to Aix, a further group made Abou Ben Adhem's tribe increase, or went Up the airy mountain, Down the rushy glen, with "The Fairies."

There must have been more interesting or modern verse but we did not know of it. We were bound by a purple book called *The Silver Treasury*, with five illustrations. After putting mustaches on the ladies' faces and scratching the name of our favorite college along the sides of the book, we settled down to a long career of recitations.

Miss Bovee sat at the end of a table with her classbook open in front of her, where all could see what marks were given. The pupil's name was called and, standing at the end of the room and facing Miss Bovee and her leering classmates, she recited. Miss Bovee closed her eyes, her lips moved silently, her facial expression changed constantly while she emphasized moods with a toss of her head.

At the conclusion, the trouble began. Miss Bovee would pick out the two most important lines and ask to have them repeated. Then she would stand up and give them herself the right way and shot with dramatics.

To the new pupil it was horrifying. She realized that to get a good mark she would have to be a damn fool; and even if she were willing to take that painful step, she did not understand the technique.

So Miss Bovee explained the "one, two, three." This meant that before the great line of the poem the pupil was to pause and count "one, two, three," and then give it everything. In "Abou Ben Adhem," the angel writes Abou's request.

The angel wrote, and vanished. The next night
It came again with a great wakening light,
And showed the names whom love of God had blessed,
And lo! [*one, two, three*] Ben Adhem's name led all the
   rest.

The "one, two, three" was at first given audibly and it was always a great struggle to say it silently, and quite impossible not to move the lips.

Miss Bovee broke down self-consciousness. She insisted on varied voices and much expression, but we were never allowed to invent our own. It must be as complete an imitation of her style as possible. "The Wreck of the Hesperus" was her great favorite. It gave rare opportunity for a deep and a high voice in the unhappy dialogue between the father and his little daughter, and it was full of "one, two, three's."

"O father! I see a gleaming light,
Oh say, what may it be?"
But the father answered never a word,
[*one, two, three*] A frozen corpse was he.

. . . .

Then the maiden clasped her hands and prayed
That savèd she might be;
And she thought [*one, two, three*] of Christ, who stilled
    the wave,
On the Lake of Galilee.

A recitation which we all learned and for which Miss
Bovee had a profound admiration was a poem by Ralph
Waldo Emerson about the mountain and the squirrel.
It was nineteen lines long and became a basic "must"
of the Always Ready members. It contained many prob-
lems.

The first was the pronunciation of the word "squirrel." As a little animal that skips up and down trees, it
remained a normal squirrel, but when it had its famous
and victorious argument with the mountain, it became
a "squi-i-rrr-il" — and woe to the girl who did not roll
it out and add an extra dot or two to the *i*'s.

The next demand was deeply embarrassing. When
the squirrel spoke, we must resemble a squirrel. This
was to be accomplished with merry eyes and an extremely roguish manner. We balked. Could we suggest

it in another way — say, by simulating nuts in our cheeks? No, we must twinkle. This was an unhappy period and the nearest I remember to mutiny. But teachers are powerful. With sulky expressions we figuratively waved our tails. Says the squi-i-rrr-il: —

If I cannot carry forests on my back,
Neither can you [*one, two, three, twinkle, dimple, and
     with great archness*] crack a nut!

There was a deep rivalry between Miss Spence, the principal of the school, and Miss Bovee over Shakespeare. Miss Spence owned Shakespeare. She had an enormous class once a week, where she read us the plays and we learned the more famous speeches.

The classes were held in the Assembly Room. We sat on camp chairs in long rows, each of us having a cloth-bound copy of the play. Miss Spence stood high above us on a platform, reading and acting and having, I always felt, the time of her life. With her there were no closed eyes, no silently moving lips. She flung herself into the parts, she loved the drunken scenes full of bad puns, but like Miss Bovee she insisted that what we learned must be given in an exact copy of her style. At a certain moment we would be made to recite some passage in unison with identical inflection.

Miss Spence was particularly fond of *The Merchant*

of Venice. For some reason which was never made clear to us, she insisted that in the opening line of Portia's great speech in the courtroom scene, the voice should rise at least an octave on the word "strained."

> The quality of mercy is not strained,
> It droppeth as the gentle rain from heaven
> Upon the place beneath.

It was not just a slight lifting of the voice: it was an enormous vocal jump. The effect of ninety girls together making this very unnatural sound never disturbed her and she would lead us like an orchestra with a swoop of her arm.

In Shylock's speech we let ourselves go and fairly shrieked, "You call me misbeliever, cut-throat, dog!" but quickly Miss Spence raised her hand. The dog, like the squirrel, had become a different animal. He was no longer a friendly Dawg: he was forever a Dahk.

Miss Spence wore voluminous, bright-colored silk dresses which had a peculiar and penetrating rustle. I have never heard a dress since that could give quite the same crackle and hiss. For us the sound was a signal to sit in an unnaturally straight position and not to turn around, thereby showing a great concentration.

Miss Spence often showed the parents of prospective pupils through the school. Once she brought a visiting father and a mother into the elocution class. Miss Bovee had unfortunately been poaching on Miss Spence's territory and had been bootlegging us some Shakespeare. The decision had to be made quickly whether to bury Caesar Miss Spence's way or Miss Bovee's. We were flustered by our audience but we were loyal to Miss Bovee.

As Caesar loved me, I weep for him; as he was fortunate, I rejoice at it; as he was valiant, I honor him; but, as he was ambitious, I slew him.

Miss Bovee felt Brutus had killed regretfully, and our voices became hushed for "slew." Miss Spence listened to two girls, but it was like a red rag to her. She stood up herself and hurled out: "But, as he was ambitious, I *slew* him!" And there was no doubt that Brutus was delighted.

Miss Bovee thanked Miss Spence and Miss Spence swished out, followed by the startled parents, who apparently were not aware of how swords had crossed. But we left Brutus for the rest of the period, and Miss Bovee after a quick blow of her nose asked for volunteers of the Always Ready Club, and her closed eyelids were pink.

At this time E. H. Sothern and Julia Marlowe were giving a cycle of Shakespeare at the Empire Theater

and we were all encouraged to go. We knew the plays
so well that we had a sense of authorship. But when
Sothern and Marlowe diverged from the interpretation
of the school, we were unanimous that they were wrong.
One mannerism of Sothern's, however, impressed me
deeply: he never said "my"; he said "meh."

> Signior Antonio, many a time and oft
> In the Rialto you have rated meh
> About meh moneys and meh usances.

This seemed to me fascinating and daring, and I was
determined, in spite of Miss Bovee, that I would never
say "my" again.

The fact that Sothern and Marlowe were married
was romantic to us, and we used to search through their
grease paint for some glint of the deep love that we
knew must be burning between them. Sothern was a
very dirty old Shylock with matted beard and sunken
eyes, and Julia Marlowe a particularly Vassar-like Portia, and they met only once in the courtroom scene, but
several girls would always claim that there had been a
moment when Shylock had looked at Portia in a "married" sort of way.

I was never convinced of this phenomenon, but when
they took their rather stately curtain calls together,
first to the right, then to the left, then to the top bal-

cony, and then to each other, surely at that moment
there was a mild, connubial glow. That was the moment when all Miss Spence's pupils broke into their
wildest applause.

At that time actors and actresses were mysterious and
remote and no magazine ever divulged their weight,
their love affairs, or how they did their manicures. But
the interest in them was just as deep, and we assumed
that as they were in their parts, so must they be in their
private lives. Half the school worshiped Maude Adams.
It was known then as a crush, but the joys of this jelly-
like state were much enhanced if they were shared by a
dozen others. Pictures of Peter Pan in his little house
in the treetops appeared inside schoolbooks to be sur-
reptitiously adored, and thimbles were worn for kisses,
and Best and Company got out a little cap with feathers. Rows of girls who were older and should have
known better excitedly waved very clean pocket handkerchiefs when Peter asked with that particular break
in his voice, "Do you believe in Fairies?" and the big
ambition was to have been to *Peter Pan* a greater number of times than anyone else.

I belonged to a smaller and more organized group
who loved William Gillette. He was then playing *Secret
Service, Held by the Enemy,* and his great role of Sherlock Holmes. The advantage of the Gillette circle, as

opposed to the Maude Adams party, lay largely in the fact that William Gillette was a man. Little girls of nine and ten adored Maude Adams. It was silly. To shiver over Sherlock Holmes in his silk dressing gown when he cried, "Quick, Watson, the needle!" bared his arm and stuck the hypodermic into the upper wrist, and then gazed out over the audience with that, oh, so tired look — that was a moment of mature experience in one's life. It made the Peter Pan goings on mere childish falderal.

We liked him best in his dusty uniform of the Union officer in *Secret Service;* in his smoking jacket; wearing his cap with the visor at each end; in his dressing gown; or as he looked when he lit his pipe. Many were the girls who at home of an evening wandered about the rooms in striped wrappers, holding imaginary pipes between their clenched teeth as they looked out wearily into the night solving little crimes.

But we were humble and we were timid. It would not have occurred to us to wait at the stage door to see William Gillette leave the theater. Instead we combined on a second-tier stage box where, if we hung far out, we could see him standing in the wings before his entrance. There was revealed to each of us in turn, by changing seats rather noisily, not Holmes, the detective, but Gillette, the man. He was equally wonderful. He looked just as tired, just as misunderstood, and just as full of dope as when he was on the stage.

We were convinced he was a real drug fiend, and in the wonderful daydreams that we wove, we forced him to give up the terrible morphine. And then came the great scene when he thanked one for having rescued him. Somehow he shed the dressing gown, was in a dusty uniform, and lo, it was a beautiful love scene.

"But I am too old for you."

"No — no — "

It ended in a vague mist and we began all over again. It was very, very silly and we were very, very happy.

Admiration for Gillette affected my elocution badly, for Gillette had a dry, almost monotonous voice admirably suited to the great Holmes but somehow lacking in the timbre necessary for Robert Browning. I would recite: —

That's meh last Duchess painted on the wall

in an ancient and weary voice and with no expression. My marks shot down but I would not give in. I felt I was at last an actress creating a role.

During the war the Office of Civilian Defense held one of its many air-raid rehearsals in which a shock feeding unit of which I was a member was asked to make a special test for speed, with all equipment. At the first wail of the siren, the group was to rush to a certain fire department and make coffee and revive the wounded firemen while doctors and first-aiders tended the other injured.

A Red Cross captain who had been sent to time us kept her eyes on her wrist watch and gave us all a real sense of panic. Four large firemen stretched themselves out on tables and cried out that they were in great agony and only a drink could save them. A little lady, a new member of the shock feeders, hidden by a too large helmet, feverishly started stirring the pot, which looked like an oversized garbage can. In it was suspended the coffee in a gauze bag surrounded by gallons of tepid water.

An elderly canteener of many courses and little experience proffered a great deal of advice. "You should have heated the water first in small quantities," she insisted.

"You've been eighteen minutes already!" announced the Red Cross captain.

"Hurry up, girls, we're bleeding to death!" yelled the firemen.

The lady, who had been murmuring some incantation at the great pot, now turned furiously.

If I cannot carry forests on my back,
Neither can you ONE, TWO, and THREE crack a nut!

The water suddenly boiled. An unknown alumna of the Always Ready Club had survived a crisis.

(4)

From the Top of the Stairs

To OBSERVE the human race and be invisible oneself gives one a strange sense of power. It is especially
interesting to study another generation and to observe
its foibles. There should be more concealed doors and
hidden balconies in the world.

We had moved to a larger and taller, high-stoop
house on Sixty-first Street which was being improved
gradually and with much discussion between my parents, while we lived in it. It possessed among other
features a long flight of stairs and from the top of it my
sisters and I watched dinner parties. It was a prosce-
nium box and gave an excellent view of a series of good
first-act entrances and exits. From our position we
could see the front hall and its mirror, the center hall
and its mirror, a section of the parlor if the portieres
were pulled back far enough, the door and a bit of the

dining room, and we had a clear view into the very congested pantry.

What we could not see, we could hear. The voices would at times be obscured; but sounds rise, and by moving down a few steps, we could catch actual dialogue.

Though the play began when the curtain went up on the cast, there was a prologue that we never missed. These fifteen minutes gave an overtone to the performance. As soon as my parents had gone down to the parlor we would seat ourselves in our box. Dressed in easy wrappers, knowing we should eat at certain intermissions, we comfortably waited for the show to start.

My mother had just opened a window, and all the portieres were waving. My father, looking very handsome in a dress suit and big white tie, hurried in.

"Margaret, it's freezing," and he lit the fire. "The papers say snow. This room gets cold enough anyhow with the draft that comes from the front door."

Then started the perennial discussion as to whether the whole house should be altered into what was called English basement. We had heard this argument so often that we turned our attention to the pantry door.

Our regular waitress, a tall lady with a great gray pompadour on the top of which rested a white cap with a black bow, was giving some directions to the hired waitress, who wore a different kind of cap and had a haughty manner. It seemed that at the last dinner party where she had hired out, she had started with the roast and the regular waitress had followed with the gravy. But Jenny, our waitress, was sticking up for her rights.

Behind them was Katy, our friend the chambermaid, who had only recently been raised in status from kitchen-maid. Katy easily broke into wild laughter if she got nervous, and showed a set of teeth that looked like Roquefort cheese. She also was wearing a cap — for the first time. Jenny considered Katy too flighty to go into the dining room, and she was kept concealed in the pantry to "hand things."

My father now appeared at the pantry door and told Katy to go in and light the candles. No matter what distance Katy had to travel, she always ran it in ten seconds flat; so seizing the matches and ejaculating an unhappy "Begorra, I'm wrong agin," she tore through the hall, not forgetting, however, to wave to us. Katy was warmhearted and wanted everyone to have a good time tonight.

There were candles on the piano, at the ends of the mantel, and in two great candelabra on the tops of the bookcases. The whole room took on a gay glow. It looked like a party. To us the depth to which the candles burned was the yardstick of how good the evening had been. If they were down a third it was average. If they burned themselves out it was tremendous.

My father's voice now came from the pantry with a note of real anguish: "Jenny, red wine is never iced! Claret should be the temperature of the room. Are you color-blind?"

There was a "Glory be to God" from Jenny, and my mother called out, "Close the pantry door. There's a smell of fish coming up through the dumb-waiter."

My father, having rectified the disaster to the claret by producing four new bottles, joined my mother again in the parlor, but his face was still flushed.

"*Ce domestique est insupportable.*"

"*Cette domestique,*" corrected my mother. She spoke better French than my father and seldom let him forget it.

My parents now began a slightly depressing discussion about their expected guests.

"The trouble with having asked Madame Henriques," said my father, "is that she spoils general conversation by wanting to tête-à-tête all the time."

My father has always been the enemy of the tête-à-tête. He hated being washed up on a sofa alone with any lady. I was never sure whether he felt that he was missing all the fun in the rest of the room or whether he felt the rest of the room was missing something good that he was saying, but he never let himself be trapped for long. An eager lady who wanted to tell him how she adored musicians never got very far unless she was willing to shout it out in front of a big circle. He wanted six or seven in on the love scene, and in the same way he felt destructive towards other duets. If a man and a woman at the dinner table seemed to be having obvious pleasure talking together, they must want to share this pleasure with everyone else. So my father would tap on his glass, propose a health, and cheerfully and successfully break up the dialogue.

"I'm sorry you asked Charley Robinson," continued my father. "He hates music."

"But I got him to balance what you told me was a French soprano, Mademoiselle Bonnard," answered my mother.

"I misread the letter of introduction. It's a tenor, René Bonnard. They say he sings very well."

"I've put him next Ethel Barrymore. Ethel will be wonderful with an unknown tenor."

"Ethel is wonderful with everyone," declared my father with great conviction, and the bell rang.

The hired waitress determinedly went to the front door and a lady came in.

"Is this Mr. Damrosch's house?" she asked.

Even to our inexperienced ears the answer did not sound quite right: "I'll be going and finding out. I'm thinking that's the name, but then agin, maybe it's not."

Jenny indignantly appeared and ushered the lady to the center hall. The hired waitress opened the front door again to a gentleman with a beard.

"It's begun to snow," he announced in a surprised voice.

We now had the double view of the lady and gentleman each in front of a mirror and both lost in contemplation. The lady finally walked into the parlor.

"Dear Madame Henriques," exclaimed my father. "What a pleasure!"

Polly beckoned us to come to the window and look out. Hundreds of little dark specks were falling by the street lamp. There was that strange soundless sound that seems to belong only to a snowstorm in the city. The pavements were white and some flakes had collected on the window sill. A taxi drew up.

Richard Harding Davis appeared in the hall below with his wife Cecil. He stood in front of the mirror looking at his handsome, ruddy, soldier-of-fortune reflection with an obvious satisfaction which we above shared. Cecil Davis was taking off a long cape. Her hair was the color of her chow dogs and she had the same mysterious eyes.

"Walter, it's begun to snow," she called.

Two other guests walked in, Irene and Charles Dana Gibson. There were loud greetings from the Davises. Dana Gibson took off his coat and hat. He had on an even bigger white tie than my father's and his collar was much higher. He looked seriously into the mirror. Then he winked at himself once and went into the center hall.

Katy, who had somehow escaped the pantry, gesticulated to us not to miss Irene Gibson. If she would only move a little closer to the mirror we could get a clear view. But in that not so very long ago ladies apparently dressed at home and did not have to remake their faces with powder and lipstick. All we could see was the tip of one white shoulder and her blond hair.

"Button this button on my glove, Dick," said Irene Gibson. "I can't get it through the hole."

My father, hearing cheerful sounds from behind the portieres, or perhaps finding himself too enmeshed by Madame Henriques, now burst through the curtains and seized the gloved hand.

"That is the host's privilege," he exclaimed.

"I got her hand first," answered Dick Davis, not letting go.

Katy, with a singular lack of tact, approached with a hairpin and said sure she could do it easy. Katy was palpably searching for any excuse to be of the party.

The doorbell rang again and they all moved into the parlor.

We watched the new arrival with interest. We had never seen him before. He carried a bouquet of roses with a ruffle of paper around it. The flowers must be for my mother. My mother must be nearly forty years old. It was preposterous. He took off his hat. Ah, good, it was an opera hat — the crush kind. We could experiment with it later. He hung up a fur-lined overcoat and unwound a heavy silk scarf from about his neck. Then to our great pleasure he pulled a small comb from an inside pocket and combed his hair carefully on each side of a middle part.

We hung over the balustrade, trying not to breathe too loud. He replaced the comb in a little case and put it back in his pocket. Suddenly he leaned forward, opened his mouth wide, and examined his teeth. Apparently satisfied, he smiled charmingly at himself, picked up the roses, and walked through the middle hall and into the parlor. Then he kissed my mother's hand.

Two more guests came and my father appeared again in the center hall, calling to Jenny to close the front door, everyone was freezing. There was a tap on the glass.

"Are you trying to shut me out?" said a lovely familiar voice.

"Ethel!" exclaimed my father with delight.

"*Ach, mein kleiner* Walter!"

He helped her off with her wrap.

"Did you know it was snowing?" she asked.

Polly signaled up to the third floor to tell Minnie, who was watching from above, to come down and get a good look. Minnie would only observe if she felt it was really worth it. Certain guests she would dismiss after a penetrating glance through her eyeglasses as "Trash!" This time she gave her highest praise.

"Very nice. Who is it?"

"It's Ethel Barrymore. Isn't she beautiful?"

Minnie studied her again. "Akee-kock, why don't they cover up their shoulders!"

Minnie was always chilly and always wore what she called a "yacket." Those who were dressed the warmest were to her the prettiest. She now turned her attention to Katy, with deep disapproval.

"Greenhorn!" Minnie hated the Irish.

From the pantry came Jenny with fourteen very small cocktail glasses in which were fourteen Bronx cocktails — no shaker, no dividends. The hired waitress followed with two plates of little sandwiches. Katy, leaping about them like a setter, opened doors and pulled curtains.

Minnie descended the stairs toward the basement.

"That tramp Antonio calls himself a furnaceman. I'm going to put on some coal myself!"

There was a series of little agony buzzes from the dumb-waiter bell. Katy lit the candles on the dining-room table and at last Jenny announced, "Dinner is served," and we watched them march into the dining room. They were all talking, the gentlemen stepping carefully so as not to walk on the ladies' trains.

Katy, having been instructed by us, partially closed the dining-room door. We ran down the stairs quickly and into the parlor. Then we drank up what was left of the cocktails. We did this because we liked the taste of orange juice and this seemed to have more bite to it than the breakfast kind. We then ate up the sandwiches.

Feeling for some reason released, we proceeded to the front hall to examine the tenor's opera hat. The fifth time that we snapped it open, it would not close. By all of us pressing it very hard together we finally shut it again. Something clicked inside. Without saying so, we knew it would never open again. We next tried on a couple of the silk hats and rubbed them both the right and the wrong way. Then we returned to our position on the stairs.

"Do ye want soup?" asked Katy.

"Skip the soup and the fish unless it's shad roe. Open

the door wider into the dining room so that we can hear."

The noise was tremendous. Everyone was talking at once. Then came my father's voice.

"Dick Davis has just asked Dana if he is not a perfect Gibson man. I insist that I have always been the model. The ladies must vote."

"I vote for Dick," cried my mother.

"Margaret, you don't count. You're prejudiced. Ethel, Irene, Cecil, I appeal to you!"

There were sounds of everyone disputing. Katy stood in the door, her mouth wide-open, watching with burning interest.

Minnie came toiling up the stairs again, carrying two plates of ice cream, one for herself and one for little Anita. She halfheartedly suggested that we go to bed.

There was applause from the dining room. Katy wheeled once, regained her sense of direction, and made for the hall.

"Sure it's your father that's won the iliction. Ain't that grand!" she panted to us.

"Hurry up and get us something to eat."

Irene Gibson was telling a darky story, mimicking each voice. There was a loud laugh, but the French tenor had apparently not understood. My father tried to translate.

"Un jour un vieux nègre s'appelait Oncle Rastu disait à son arrière petit-fils — "

"You had better say it in German," urged my mother.

"Es war einmal ein alter schwarzer Mann," obliged my father, *"der bei dem Name Onkle Rastus bekannt war. . . ."*

As the dinner progressed, the noise from the dining room grew louder and louder and sounded like the lions at feeding time. We could no longer distinguish conversation.

We ate sections of the courses as they were brought to us, a mélange of salad, rolls, cake, and Hollandaise sauce. The dessert was an egg shape of yellow ice cream embedded in a nest of spun sugar. The spun sugar did not possess any particular flavor, but, like alligator pears, was a party dish we always hailed with admiration. It scratched the mouth but looked holiday. Polly placed some on her upper lip in a trailing white mustache and signaled to the faithful public, Katy.

"Ye look just like Santa Claus," she called appreciatively.

A pleasant smell of tobacco smoke began to float up the stairs. A little later the ladies left the gentlemen, but Cecil Davis remained in the dining room.

"That's what I'm going to do," I announced. "I'm

always going to stay with the men and never join the ladies."

I saw a rosy future — me, in a train, with yellow hair, sitting at a table surrounded by Gibson profiles in white ties.

As the men walked through the center hall looking well-fed and contented, Madame Henriques came through the portieres.

"I think I left my handkerchief in my wrap," she said to my father.

"Let me help you."

Madame Henriques seemed to be in no hurry to find it.

"When I watched you conduct last Friday I was so profoundly moved. There was a certain something — "

"It was the tails of my beautiful new dress suit," replied my father, spreading them out. "Jenny," and he made for the pantry door, "bring in the Scotch."

Madame Henriques was left hunting her handkerchief.

The door upstairs opened and little Anita, eluding Minnie and dressed in a pair of blue flannel pajamas, joined us.

"It's snowing!" she told us.

We went again to the window. An unmistakable sound came from outdoors, the scrape of a wooden shovel. There was no one on the streets, but down the block two men had begun to pile the snow. It was a real blizzard. Already the footprints of the guests on our steps had been obliterated. We opened the windows. The outside world had changed. It was intoxicating watching the white flakes whirl by. We must be the only people awake in the city to see it.

Then we heard my father playing a few soft chords at the piano, and the voice of Bonnard rang out: —

> *O, mon enfant, ma soeur,*
> *Songe à la douceur*
> *D'aller là-bas vivre ensemble.*

The voice was beautiful, with that strange intensity that seems to be the unique possession of French singers.

"He's good," whispered Anita.

He sang on: —

> *Là, tout n'est qu' ordre et beauté*
> *Luxe, calme et volupté.*

Across the street a taxi drew up, struggling through the drifts. Our neighbor, Mrs. Douglas Robinson, was coming home from a party with some friends, and their shouts and laughter echoed across to us as they floundered through the snow.

Up the stairs came the creaking footsteps of the cook, who was carrying a loud ticking clock and groaning to herself. Again we heard the piano, and Monsieur Bonnard sang: —

> *Voici des fruits, des fleurs,*
> *Des feuilles et des branches,*
> *Et puis voici mon coeur* . . .

We knew that the candles would gut themselves tonight.

5

"Will the Young Ladies Take Partners . . ."

Outside Activities, as they were called, meant the culture and beauty which could not be found within the walls of the school from nine to one o'clock. The activities consisted of music lessons, dancing school, going to museums, and Health, which meant walking in Central Park and visits to the dentist. The dentist worked like an electrician, wiring teeth front and back, and it was quite unfashionable not to have in your mouth a lot of fancy things which had to be tightened every two weeks.

Parents were as diabolic then as now at beating the game, and adroitly worked out a system of killing two birds. On the long trips by streetcar in the search for aesthetic frills, the child was accompanied by a governess trying to force a rapid conversation in a foreign

language. An exhausted little girl would return home
in the evening with both a new brace and the *passé
antérieur* fixed in her jaws. Then she had her supper,
tried to whistle through the latest addition to her teeth,
and did homework.

Miss Spence held two activities during the school
hours. The first was called Gym, and took place once
a week for half an hour. A visiting lady gymnast appeared in a pair of enormous black satin bloomers. The
girls then marched in columns about the assembly
room to music from *Le Prophète*. For eight minutes
she led them in calisthenics, which were done very
gently with the arms, to a waltz. Then everyone skipped
to a polka, and Athletics were over for another seven
days.

The other activity was Art. School art never changes
much. We drew a pear next to a plate, in charcoal.
We made the shadows by smudging the charcoal darkly
with our thumbs; we made a high light on the pear
and the plate by rubbing two neat white spots with
a soft eraser. We had two weeks' instruction in wet
wash, in clay, in bookplate designing. Our parents received the results as Christmas gifts. In the spring there
was an exhibit at which each child stood blushing beside "Design in Batik," "Original Drawing," "Poem in
Gothic Lettering," "Glazed Placque for Paperweight."

Art was not a heartbreak for perfection, filled with Left Bank yearnings. It was fun.

My sister and I had first music lessons on West 85th Street. To get there we took three streetcars and climbed four flights of stairs. Mrs. Stagman had a special system of instruction. Her first command after greeting us was, "Take an apple." We each took an apple and gripped it, and then, removing the apple but keeping the hand in the gripping position, transferred it to the piano. A quarter was then placed on the back of the hand and we were told that we were now in the correct position for the piano. We went twice a week on this journey for the apple, and it took my father several months to realize that we were not bounding ahead as he had expected. We were then transferred to the Institute of Musical Art.

Uncle Frank Damrosch was the head of the Institute and it was the most important and serious school of music in the country. Among its pupils then and later were: Risë Stevens, Yehudi Menuhin, and Richard Rodgers. The students were studying to become professional artists and were working long hours. The Institute was at the opposite end of the city, in a beautiful old building near Washington Square. It took half an hour by streetcar to get there. Into this scholastic and serious atmosphere, Polly and I bounded one day as the youngest pupils, in Peter Thompson sailor suits.

We were beginning to be faintly aware that learning to play the piano meant work, and so we optimistically hoped that, as our uncle ran the school, it would be a family affair, and he would in a friendly way not expect too much of that practicing nonsense. We associated him with lighting the tree at Christmas and with other happy occasions. We expected the spirit of holiday cheer would continue. We were quickly disappointed.

My uncle welcomed us and then expressed his high hopes for us. This had an ominous sound. He introduced us to our teacher, Miss J., who was a little startled by our small size but concluded, I think, that we must be prodigies. She was a very serious lady, dedicated to the cause of music and believing that one must begin with fundamentals.

She started us immediately on harmony and counterpoint and wrote some notes rapidly on a blackboard by way of illustration. She then presented us with two musical notebooks and told us that we would begin by working on simple composition. Making black dots and hooking tails onto them seemed easy, and we learned to draw very beautiful clefs.

After a few weeks Miss J. hopefully gave us the as-

signment of an original theme with variations, to be
written first in the major and then the minor key. Not
being quite sure what "original theme" meant, I stole
the tune of "*Ach, du lieber Augustin*" and brought it
carefully transcribed with one major chord at the beginning and a strange, sour chord at the end. Miss J.
played it, added a few harmonies of her own, and tact-
fully did not accuse me of plagiarism.

Polly then placed her composition on the piano. It
was several pages long, and written with very black
pencil. Miss J. looked, and looked again. There were
quarter notes, trills, chords, sharps, flats, and a number of written commands and suggestions as to interpretation. "A *tempo, ritard, fortissimo, più, più, più,
mosso.*" Miss J. left the room and returned with my
uncle, who was carrying the composition. He looked
perturbed, but he loved Polly.

"Tell me," he began, "this Tone Poem that you have
written must have been quite difficult."

"Oh, no," said Polly looking like a modest Mozart,
"it went very fast."

"Here for instance there are four whole notes in one
measure and the key is indicated by two flats and three
sharps. I am not familiar with that key. You do not
find it necessary as a composer to follow the rules of
harmony laid down by Miss J.?"

The answer was evasive. "Sometimes I do, and sometimes I don't."

"And did you write this at the piano?"

"I wrote it all," cried Polly triumphantly, "in the Madison Avenue streetcar!"

"Ah," said my uncle, and he eyed the composition again. "If you will let me keep this, I think I will show it to your dear father. Pianistically the problems you present will interest him. Now why don't we all leave Miss J. and listen to a very good recital of Schumann. He is not so intricate a composer, but we think that, in a small way, he had talent too. By the way, Polly, haven't you lost another tooth?"

My uncle transferred us from Miss J. to a humbler teacher who with cynical realism started us learning to play the scale of C.

I have often wondered why the rate of suicide among music teachers is not higher. It is a dreadful thing to know how beauty sounds, and then to hear it hammered out in all shapes and forms. My sisters and I in the next few years raised an army of piano teachers as large as Kitchener's Mob. Polly was the only one who really played well and deserved the efforts of that gallant group that we successively broke.

My father was too busy with his own career to do more than jump in and out in the role of adviser. If we were not good enough to become professionals, and that meant really good, he was not interested in having us become amateurs. Schools were always making the major demand of time for homework; music meant hours of practicing. In that age-old tug of war, the music teachers lost.

We wanted to go to dancing school. We loved to dance, but our dancing was an inventive form of our own, and we wanted to learn "steps." My mother entered us in Tanief's Dancing School.

Mr. Tanief, a Russian with large, muscular legs, believed in a very expressive form of the art full of folklore and symbolism. He requested us to buy ballet slippers and tambourines. His own tambourine was decorated with many bright silk streamers and he urged us to adorn ours also. My mother, either becoming a little depressed as each new art that her daughters espoused entailed more and more equipment, or perhaps economically feeling she had done enough by us with the ballet slippers, gave us each only one ribbon. In the tarantella our tambourines looked like forlorn polliwogs with long red tails, and we never could make her understand why this was so peculiar.

Mr. Tanief so loved to dance that most of the hour was taken up in his showing us how to do it and then waiting impatiently until he could spring in again among us with a great bound and dance some more himself. He would weave in and out, his arms outstretched and his eyes not fastened critically upon our legs and arms, but on some far-off audience in St. Petersburg. If we clapped him when he clicked his heels three times together in the air, he would disappear and then run out and bow to us with the great manner of the star acknowledging his public.

When a parent appeared to see how a child was progressing, to Mr. Tanief it was a new audience. He would put on a performance of "The Wedding Feast" or "The Sword Dance," whirling about well to the front himself and allowing the pupils to assume graceful but stationary poses in the background. This was very charming, but if a mother still insisted on a sample of her daughter's progress, Mr. Tanief would call the child to him, place his hand on her head, and say: "Yes, yes. Art is long. We understand each other. Is it not?"

But I wanted to go to a regular dancing school. The desire to be a sheep with the sheep was already becoming my major ambition, and in a city of five millions there was, I felt, only one place to learn to dance: where my friends from school went — Dodworth's Dancing School. More than that, I told my mother, with a trembling lip, I could not possibly be seen there unless

I had a pair of high white kid buttoned boots. More equipment, but my patient mother bought them for me.

If Mr. Tanief's dream was to perform before the Tsar and receive a decoration from him, Mr. Dodworth saw himself sitting in the kingly loge with the Tsarina and conferring the honor. He was a complete royalist, not merely at heart, but with every fiber of his being. His great ambition was to bring back the minuet.

Though the classes were held every afternoon, Thursday was felt to be The Day, and when a girl first joined, Mrs. Dodworth quickly wrote the mother that Mr. Dodworth would consider it desirable if she came twice a week.

When a girl entered the ballroom, she dropped a court curtsy. Mr. Dodworth and his assistant, both in what is called faultless evening attire and with white kid gloves, responded with deep bows. She then slid across the floor — it was against the rule ever to walk — and joined her friends. They sat in long rows, a mass of curls, hair ribbons, party dresses, and all wearing high white kid buttoned boots and long white kid gloves. From this part of the room there was wafted into the air a considerable smell of naphtha, for the kid shoes and gloves had to be constantly cleaned.

The boys, also in white gloves, and wearing pumps,

were on the opposite side. The pumps were always a little loose and were easily kicked about. At the end of the ballroom, on a little raised platform, sat Mrs. Dodworth in full evening dress, with a black aigrette in her hair, writing at a little French desk presumably our very expensive bills. On the desk was a vase with a single pink rose.

We learned the waltz, the boston, the lancers, the schottische, the quadrille, and Mr. Dodworth's chef-d'oeuvre, the minuet. This was danced very stiffly and cautiously, with a good deal of balancing and peering at each other through curved arms and delicately bent wrists.

We began with the waltz, practicing it in a square and then dancing it without a partner about the ballroom. Then came an announcement. "Will the young ladies take partners for the Waltz and the Reverse." This was a big moment. Tremblingly the girls grabbed each other and started out at first painfully and then with a kind of gamboling boldness. The little boys seized victims and tried to race each other and see who could cover most ground and cut corners fastest. At the dizzy signal for the Reverse the partner would give a yank which was the cue. We would then struggle to unwind ourselves, in a left-handed and unnatural effort to go "the wrong way."

At some point as we first danced about the room we were supposed to stop for a split second and greet Mrs. Dodworth. Etiquette did not require the court curtsy, but a shorter knix. This knix was always made by every little girl when she shook hands with an older person, and it became such an automatic reflex of bending the knee with giving the hand that it took great physical discipline to discard it as one grew older. Many girls when they were fifteen or sixteen would make the embarrassing error of knixing to contemporaries of the opposite sex.

There were two ambitions. The first was never to dance with a boy if it could be avoided. There were only about a fourth as many boys as girls. They obviously did not want to be there, and their protest consisted in dancing as badly as possible and being "funny." They were frequently reprimanded by Mr. Dodworth, who began those little talks with a demand for complete silence and then addressed them as "Young gentlemen — if you still deserve the name!" The girls shuddered at this taunt, but the boys never seemed to mind.

The second ambition was to get into the third class, second division. No boy ever got beyond the second class, but when a girl reached the point of being tapped for this exalted group, it was done with considerable ceremony. Mr. Dodworth invited the anointed one to dance with him. She dropped a low, grateful curtsy and with a pale face waltzed rigidly in Mr. Dodworth's arms, held seven inches from his beautiful white shirt. At the conclusion he pinned a pale blue ribbon on her chest, on which was printed, strangely enough, "The Golden Rule." Then, suffused with blushes, she slid back to her seat.

At this time the first faint drumbeats of the jazz age had begun to sound through the land with "Alexander's Ragtime Band." There were rumors, hints, that something exciting was happening, and feet were beginning to tap, tap in a very unorthodox way. Mr. Dodworth — who was, to say the least, a traditionalist — was squarely on record that only the boston and a kind of watered one-step would receive his sanction. And he still had his dream for the minuet.

Mr. Dodworth was, I think, very gallant to have had such high ambitions, but outside his little ballroom a different world had begun to roar. There was the Dip. In the boston the lady suddenly dipped deep down to the floor with her back leg well extended, and the deeper she dipped, the more she was admired. Mr. Dodworth forbade the Dip.

Then came a great dish of forbidden fruit: the lame duck, the turkey trot, the bunny hug, and the notorious grizzly bear. At school during recess, younger girls watched wide-eyed as juniors and seniors began showing each other the intricacies of these dances. In the lame duck one foot trailed after the other in a big limp; the turkey trot was very fast; the bunny hug I do not remember; but the grizzly bear was very slow and demanded a certain heaving of the shoulders of the partners in unison.

This was too much for Mr. Dodworth. He made us a warning speech telling us how we would be letting him down if we ever in our lives were caught doing "these modern gyrations." He gave a humorous imitation of how we would look and we laughed courteously, as expected. In conclusion he remarked significantly: "Shoulders were intended for quite another purpose!"

As we put on our velvet carriage shoes over our kid boots, we pondered over this. What future role was the shoulder to play in our lives? It was just another of the mysteries that were beginning to crowd in on us. There were so many things that were never explained.

6

Oh! Oh! That Gaby, Gaby Glide

DANCING school was a lighthearted affair but it was a preparation for the big event, Real Dances with Boys. These did not start for us officially until we were about fifteen, but the shadow no bigger than a black tie was already faintly on the horizon.

I came back to school in the autumn full of my summer experiences. I had got into the second round of a tennis tournament; I had broken my arm, an important and interesting event. My friends were talking of something quite different — boys. The summer had changed them. It was now October 2. They were already speaking of the Christmas holidays. They had mysterious jokes. Things had happened to them. They had moved on into a different world. I wanted to be part of the world and show that things had happened to me too.

I had had one adventure, but I was not certain that it measured up to the momentous experiences of my friends. I was driving the buggy from the village of Westport on Lake Champlain to our summer home. It was twilight and the evening was full of fireflies. I had sunk into that coma, so frequent at fourteen, when you have to be addressed several times by name before you hear and answer. You are Thinking. Suddenly a boy appeared along the road, gave a piercing whistle and then said, but softly, "Oh, you kid!" Convention demanded that I do one of two things: whip up the horse, or answer with quick repartee, "Twenty-three — Skiddoo!" I did neither. I allowed the horse to go more slowly, hoping faintly that the boy might say it again. He didn't.

Some of the girls had letters and they were reading them in whispers — bits of them, not all — to each other. I remember my sense of bleakness. It would never be quite the same again. A girl none of us liked very much was treated with deference. In the summer she had danced with boys who were already in college — college men. She was a belle. Why was she? Other girls had just as pretty dresses. She wore a somewhat

larger bow on the back of her hair than the rest of us.
And college men wanted to dance with her. Every
value shifted. Friendships were realigned. Adam was
entering Eden to destroy its peace forever.

The girls who had brothers had an advantage and
fared the best. They were used to their brothers' friends
and took it more lightheartedly. But to those who did
not possess this valuable relative, it was a terrifying
time. We were told often a girl must never lose the
respect of a member of the opposite sex. Come hell or
high water, one must be respected. What was this respect? It was again vague; one started with it and then
under no circumstances apparently could lose it. But
did our school friend with the big bow, who had such
a lively time, always receive this melancholy tribute?
We were not so sure.

So at fifteen, profoundly worried and full of respect,
we began what we were fully convinced was the most
desperate time of our lives. In New York it was not easy
to see boys. There were no movies, no outdoor events.
There were a few dances, Sunday calls, and an occasional matinee.

The boys from the fourth form up were all addressed
as Mister. They called the girls Miss. This went on for

months. Then came what was felt to be "the moment" for first names. This was a fascinating problem. Should you ask the boy to call you by your first name, or should he, or might it just happen? When it occurred it was Chapter VII of Romance.

But before any of this could happen, the girls had to meet boys — the first great hurdle. There were in New York then, as there are today, subscription dances for the girls, to which they each invited two boys. The question then arose, "What boys?" Your cousin was away and your friends' brothers frightened you.

My mother, with good intentions, announced that one of her friends had sons and she would write her friend to deliver them up. This was full of dreadful possibilities. Mothers always seemed vague as to the ages of boys and might make a bad mistake of three years either way. Every girl knew from long experience that no one ever gets on with the children of her parents' friends. If they were attractive and the right age they would already have been bespoken. If they came they would be "pills" and think that you were a "lemon." These were the only two words used to describe social failures.

An elaborate correspondence began between the mothers, then further letters to the young men — who were of course protesting and were only too convinced they were getting into something bad. I suppose this was the ancestor of the Blind Date. When the situation became too desperate the fathers were appealed to. Bad-tempered New York lawyers — they were bad-tempered then, they are bad-tempered now — would order their exhausted junior partners to "be at that ballroom at nine-thirty and God damn it you dance with Helen!" I found myself with a medical student, and my father produced a young man called Albert Spalding for my sister Polly.

The stag line at the first dance would be as varied as the draft. Little boys who had just got their long pants would stand beside tired Wall Street men doing their duty by the Old Man's daughter.

By the second or third dance it had shaken down. We had begun to know boys of the right age. One could launch out on one's own and start a romantic correspondence with a member of the opposite sex.

NEW YORK, *November 1st,* 1912

DEAR MR. RUSSELL,

Will you come to the first Holiday dance with me on December 18th? Laura Henry is having a dinner first, and if you can come, her mother will send you an invitation.

Yours sincerely,

GRETCHEN B. DAMROSCH

ST. MARK'S SCHOOL, SOUTHBORO, MASS.
December 8th, 1912

DEAR MISS DAMROSCH,

I am sorry but school doesn't let out until December 20th which cuts me out of the Holiday.

Sincerely yours,

FREDERICK J. RUSSELL III

This answer was carefully preserved. It was a Letter from a Boy.

If things went well with Mr. Russell but did not reach Chapter VII quickly enough, one might be excessively bold.

DEAR FRED (I just can't call you Mr. any more!),

Will you come to the Easter Holiday, etc. etc.

The chaperon today is almost as much of a costume piece as the Duenna Marianne in *Der Rosenkavalier*. But then she was a reality. She was in the next room and buzzed in and out to make everyone know she was there, she sat in the extra seat at the theater, she appeared veiled and protected at football games, she waited endlessly in cabs and cars. She was preferably married, but could be single if she was the spinster type. A play of the day — I think it was *The College Widow* — had a very alluring character for this role and the second-act curtain line was, "What I demand to know is, who is chaperoning the chaperon!" This was considered uproarious and made parents even more determined to have "settled" women to protect their daughters.

If a girl protested too fiercely and demanded the reason for all this shadowing, she received the answer: "Because I do not wish my daughter to be considered fast."

To be "fast" had various interpretations. It meant going out alone with one or more boys. It meant putting powder on one's face. It meant smoking. It meant giving the impression that one was in "high spirits." High spirits with a young man meant drink, and with a girl meant a cheerful acceptance of his condition.

My sister Alice had a friend at Yale who came from Evanston, Illinois. He had a very serious approach to life, and he and Alice discovered that they both believed in Platonic friendship. They were much interested in the subject and they would sit on a sofa in the firelight discussing the whole question.

They also exchanged a number of earnest letters on the problem. As Alice wrote, "There is no earthly reason why real friendship should not exist between a man and a woman, or even a boy and a girl, without all that sentimental slush which honestly interferes, don't you think? I should really like to know your frank opinion on this."

The Yale man assured her that he thought her attitude quite wonderful "in this day and age," that he had hoped all his life for Platonic friendship, had never until now found it, was coming down to New York for the Harding dance, and how about going to the theater with him first.

My mother proved very narrow in her attitude, refused to recognize that this was a new relationship, and still insisted that there must be a chaperon. So Alice wrote that she would like to go to *The Dollar Princess* because everyone said Donald Brian was marvelous, but it would be necessary to get three tickets because of the old chaperon nonsense.

This was the Yale man's first unpleasant shock. At Evanston you just took a girl out. The next surprise was much more painful. He arrived the day of the party and went to the box office, as he would have at home, to buy the tickets. There were none to be had. He consulted friends who laughed at him. He became the true bulldog and finally got them through a broker for eighteen dollars apiece. This so reduced his funds that instead of procuring an orchid, as he had planned, he sent Alice sweet peas surrounded by asparagus fern.

The chaperon, a friend of my mother's, belonged to

the nineteenth century, the age of sentiment, and assumed that this charming young man must be courting Alice. She was very, very tactful, and read her program over and over again while occasionally throwing an understanding and sympathetic glance to the Yale man over what she felt was the loveliest moment in young people's lives. She did not know about Plato.

Apparently the combination of events was too much. There was Alice, covered with pink sweet peas, who apparently found Donald Brian particularly handsome, there was this arch old lady, and he was out fifty-four dollars. For the next holiday he returned to Evanston.

The dances were held at old Sherry's, which had two ballrooms. The small ballroom was the scene of our ecstasy. It was lined with mirrors, it had rose silk curtains, and it had a place to sit out, with palms.

Each girl was accompanied and called for by a maid, and in the dressing room sat a row of these pale and sleepy creatures. I have often wondered how they were ever persuaded to perform so fatiguing a job.

When a girl arrived in the dressing room, she spent many minutes "prinking" her marcelled hair. Then she put talcum powder — secretly brought from home concealed in absorbent cotton in a little bag — on her nose. Snow-white noses were considered very dashing.

Then she stood, hesitating. But the music was playing "Oh! Oh! That Gaby, Gaby Glide." It was irresistible. With a beating heart she rapidly shook hands with a row of patronesses and entered the ballroom.

When we first went to dances, dancing was so exciting that nobody wanted to sit out. The ballroom was always crowded. Then again came one of those divisions. We saw the fast girls, on whom our jealous eyes were always fixed, sitting on little sofas, having long heart-to-hearts with intent young men. The ballroom suddenly emptied. The palm trees became jammed. Everyone started sitting out. It was considered "young" to dance so hard and so enthusiastically.

Mr. Conrad was the favorite orchestra leader. His music was never too loud, and the most awkward kept time to his beat. He had a dark mustache which gradually whitened through the years, but he never lost the glint in his eye and he gave style to every party. He also did not forget names, and young men were immensely flattered when he recognized them.

"Play 'The Pink Lady' once again, Mr. Conrad."

"Give us 'Naughty Marietta.' "

Card dances and cotillions presented hazards. On the card were engraved perhaps sixteen dances. In the middle was a break, which was the supper dance. After the final dance came three "extras." To the card was at-

tached a little pencil by a silken cord. The young men
were supposed to seize the pencil in a masterful way
and write down what they wanted. The most significant
dances were the first, the supper, and the last extra. It
was a little like a letter, the end being the most important part, though the beginning gave a clue to the
contents.

A belle who was receiving several rushes had her card
filled the fastest. The poor lemons with fixed smiles on
their unhappy faces often wrote false initials after One-
Step and Tango so as not to discourage possible bidders.

No one has described the sufferings of a girl with
greater genius or poignancy than Booth Tarkington in
Alice Adams. The agony of Alice is ageless, and her pa-
thetic efforts to make the others at the party feel she
belonged and was desired still make the sweat break
out on my forehead.

A girl's only sin may have been shyness. But what
tortures she endured if a dance was not taken or she had
been "stuck" too long. She would disappear into the
dressing room and prink her hair. If only her friends
would not see her. With a glassy smile for the benefit of
the row of maids, she faced the mirror wondering desperately how to secure another partner. The memory of
a terrible song came to her. How did I "pick a lemon in
the Garden of Love, where they say only peaches grow"?

She must get home. But even if she finally managed to steal out, she had the last hurdle of passing her parents' door, from behind which a sleepy voice invariably called out, "Did you have a good time?"

"Wonderful!" was the inevitable answer. How could she explain?

At the cotillions the girls were loaded with paper caps and ruffs, jingle bells and parasols. The boys received boutonnieres of red roses, sashes, feathers. If the party was very grand, the favors became elaborate — beaded evening bags and fans of the then fashionable sandalwood. The boys received sandalwood cigarette cases and real pipes.

Of course there was competition to be the most favored, and girls kept their paper and silk trophies hung about their mirrors for months. A giant sunflower which looked as though it had been through a sandstorm was there to remind a girl, when she lifted her eyes from homework, of a better world.

Boys liked the afternoon *Thés Dansants* — pronounced Tee Dance-Ants. They did not feel bound by duty dances; they did not have to dress up. They went in droves, usually bringing along eight or ten uninvited classmates apiece. The orchestra was made up of three colored gentlemen, one a drummer. The drummer was always surrounded by a large, respectful circle of fifth-

and sixth-formers. At the party he received the most attention. The punch bowl and food were second; the
girls ran a poor third.

Parents, who were not supposed to appear at dances,
often dropped in at the *Thés Dansants* and sat along the
walls watching their sons and daughters. This was re-
pressing but there seemed to be nothing to do about it.
The parents were so innocently happy to be allowed to
look on. Then fate intervened in a strange way.

We had been in Paris the summer before. There was
a new dance called the maxixe. It had a heel-and-toe
step, a skating step, a bending step, and very good music.
We had three fifteen-franc lessons and were taught to
perform it in a grim but efficient manner.

One afternoon we went to a party at the Pré-Catelan.
The orchestra was playing a soggy tango and young
South-American-looking men were leading out elderly
and dressy ladies in a series of intricate steps. We knew
that this was Life in the French capital, but it was
somehow depressing. No one smiled.

Suddenly there was a roll of the drums and the floor
was cleared. The orchestra began a gay polka and out
came a young man with a hawk face, walking very jaunt-
ily in rhythm while in his arms floated a girl with
bobbed curly hair on which sat a little Dutch cap. Their
feet did not seem to touch the ground and they were

both laughing. Their gaiety swept the room like an electric breeze. The music quickened; the walk became a skip, faster and faster.

The room broke into wild applause. They returned again and danced a maxixe but in double time and with a great deal of snap, both of them still laughing. At the conclusion there were cheers. In eight minutes this couple had destroyed forever the solemnity of dancing.

The lightness and grace of the girl, the skill of the man, and above all their gaiety, made all those at the little tables want to jump up and recapture for themselves something so young and happy. The tango was thrown out of the window. The Vernon Castles had arrived and were to become the rage of two continents.

In the winter they appeared in New York in a musical called *Watch Your Step*. They had the same effect on their audiences. Older people took up dancing. When the music of "Little girl, mind how you go" sounded, with one accord the parents crowded onto dance floors, shoving children aside as they *skipped* up and down ballrooms, tipping inward around corners at a forty-five-degree angle to keep their balance. Nothing could stop them; nothing could hold them down. From eight to eighty, led by the whirling feet of Vernon and Irene Castle, the whole world went dance-mad. And then from eight to eighty the ladies began to bob their hair.

7

Two Performances

M Y FATHER has always felt that members of a family should help each other. He has frequently bailed out his daughters and in turn has expected us to help him when the going was hard.

My father's requests never were strange to him; for, being a man of great imagination, he saw a plan beautiful and whole, which might need only a little assistance here and there. But to us he seemed not always to recognize the realities.

My father liked doing the new works of composers, and they in turn were eager to have him perform their compositions, for he respected their intentions, did not cut, and gave a beautiful and inspired reading. Many years ago he invited Tschaikowsky to come to New York and conduct some of his own works at the opening of a new auditorium for music, Carnegie Hall. Tschaikowsky dined frequently at my parents' home, and my father often described to us his gentle conversation, which was permeated with a kind of sadness.

The following summer my father went to England, to Cambridge University, to attend the presentation of degrees to five composers from five different countries: Saint-Saëns of France, Boïto of Italy, Grieg of Norway, Bruch of Germany, and Tschaikowsky of Russia. At the great banquet in the evening Tschaikowsky, next to whom my father sat, described a new symphony which he had just finished and which was different in form from anything he had written before.

"The last movement," said Tschaikowsky, "is an adagio and the whole work has a program."

"Tell me the program," begged my father.

"That, I shall never tell anyone," replied Tschaikowsky. "But I shall send to you the first orchestral score and parts."

In October came the cable that Tschaikowsky had died of cholera; but one week later the score and orchestra parts of the great Symphony Number 6, the "Pathétique," arrived from Moscow for my father. Through the years, audiences when listening to this profound and moving work have had to ponder for themselves what the "program" was that Tschaikowsky had intended but never revealed.

My father liked taking chances with unknown young composers, and no matter what the demands were in the score, he provided the opportunity for the work to be heard. If it was an opera and he had no opera company at the time, he gave it in concert form; if the instrumentation called for fourteen harps, fourteen harpists were procured.

One day my sisters and I heard a new and irresistible kind of music coming up the stairs from the living room. We were drawn as by a magnet to the sounds. Seated at the piano was a young man with black hair and an engaging smile, puffing at a cigar as he played a melody that made one want to laugh with pleasure.

My father introduced us to George Gershwin; and though we did not know it, that introduction began for us some of the gayest years of our lives. My father asked Gershwin to write him something for the orchestra, and the "Concerto in F" resulted. Later at Gershwin's request he gave the first performance of "An American in Paris."

My father liked dramatic productions. Besides a good orchestra and singers, he liked a chorus, costumes, scenery, make-up, spotlights, rehearsals, opening nights. He liked the works and he had uncanny power of pulling a show together. He was greatly interested in the technical end of a production and quickly established a blood brotherhood with a scene painter or wig man. He admired their skill; they liked his praise and they were always willing to change this or that to suit him. If a problem seemed insurmountable he would enjoy discovering some new craftsman who would find himself a sort of partner of my father's in making blacker smoke for the dragon's mouth or a longer sword to be welded.

Though most of a production is created in studios or draftsmen's ateliers, my father wanted as much as possible to be done in our home. He had ideas that he wanted to see carried out, and it seemed simpler to concentrate everything under one roof. He liked the singers to have extra rehearsals there; he liked costumes to be made then and there under his eyes; he liked to look at sketches of battlements and move the fort over from stage right to stage left; and he particularly liked to confer with electricians.

I do not know how my mother stood it. Like a tidal wave, rooms would fill up with tenors, medieval capes, scores to which were attached a copyist who needed an extra-large table, an assistant conductor, a ballet master, a photographer, while the piano never stopped sounding. If the group came in the morning, they stayed for lunch. If they rehearsed in the evening, they had a late supper. And no people eat so heartily as musicians. They are like athletes in top condition who break training every few hours.

Even when I was very young, certain words were already familiar to me though I did not clearly understand their meaning. There was a thing called "professional rates," and two ominous creatures named "The Union" and "Overtime." These ferocious animals seemed to be always lurking about, trying to destroy rehearsals. Their lair was a place called Local 802; and the older they grew, the stronger they apparently became.

When my sisters and I were connected with a production, we did as we were told and were usually amenable. Anita, however, occasionally had the courage to defy my father. Sometimes there seemed to be a jinx on us, and our part of a performance went awry. Twice mishaps occurred in *The Children of Bethlehem*. This opera by Gabriel Pierné is a little masterpiece musically and dramatically. In simple and poetic terms it tells the story of the children and shepherds following the Star to the stable at Bethlehem. They join a procession headed by the three Kings, and all present their gifts to the Child Jesus.

My father gave this opera at the New Theater. Besides the singers, he had eight professional children for a small chorus. Polly and I were among the eight professionals. We received a dispensation from school, and we rehearsed both at home and at the theater. We used

our professional rating to the limit, opened no schoolbooks, and talked boastfully to our friends of the exhausting life behind the footlights.

At this time the real professional children were creatures apart. Not only could they sing and act, but they
could dance on the tips of their toes, whistle, and turn
cartwheels. They were never frightened. They could repeat a scene over and over again with complete assur-
ance. Polly and I were filled with a dreadful shyness.
Not so the other children.

But when they acted, they were children imitating
middle-aged men and women acting like children. They
had studied artlessness. They were gay or surprised in
the correct technical way to express these emotions.
Perhaps the charm of children lies in their doing
things because they feel like it and occasionally making
mistakes. Never did these little professionals give a spon-
taneous gesture or go wrong. They were prompt in their
cues, and they remembered exactly how they had been
directed.

When the Star of Bethlehem appeared, Polly and I
would show our admiration differently at each rehearsal,
usually by opening our mouths wide and gaping, but we
never quite remembered how we had done it before.
The six others learned what to do and never varied. Two
would put their arms about each other and skip a little,

another would raise her hands above her head and clap them three times as she took two steps forward. We really were children but didn't know how to put it over so that the balcony would murmur, "Aren't they *darling!*"

There was one girl whom Polly and I regarded with a mixture of jealousy and envy. Her name was Tina Varesi and she was the daughter of a very successful Italian grocer. Tina had long yellow hair, and Mrs. Varesi, who accompanied her everywhere, would pass a comb through Tina's locks if there was as much as a moment's pause in the rehearsal. Tina had a clear, high soprano, sang well, and had acted since she was a baby. We envied her her life. She slept late in the morning, sat up late at night, and only once in a while went to school. We glossed over the fact that she spoke four languages and had a dancing and singing lesson every day.

Mrs. Varesi kept Tina apart from the other children, since she felt that Tina was almost a leading lady and must be treated in a special way. As we were the daughters of the conductor we could talk to her, but we bored Tina.

The soprano who sang the part of the Virgin particularly liked Tina. She found all Tina's little tricks very endearing, and when she motioned the children to draw nearer with their gifts for the little Jesus, she always gave her a warm smile. This was a very beautiful moment in the opera. It was posed like a medieval painting. Several steps led up to a little platform which was a part of the stable. On the platform sat the Virgin near the manger; behind her were the heads of the Ox and the Ass looking through their stalls. After the offerings had been made by the children, the three Wise Men approached with their gifts. Then the entire cast, including the Ox and the Ass, sang the great chorus of the opera.

The day before the performance, my father asked the children to bring from home some simple toy, a fruit, or a vegetable to carry as their gifts. Mrs. Varesi listened carefully, as she always did to anything that might concern Tina's role, and nodded her head vigorously.

"*Si, si*, Mr. Damrosch. Leave it to me," and she passed her comb once more through Tina's hair. My father patted Tina's head, and Tina immediately assumed the correct pose of a child being patted on the head by an older man. She parted her lips and looked eager and grateful.

I planned to bring an old doll, and Polly, who was to be dressed as a boy and was deeply interested in her part, told my mother to get her a lot of brightly colored fruits which she could place in twos and threes at the foot of the cradle.

"Yes, yes," said my mother absent-mindedly, "I'll have them there."

No matter how often artists have openings, they are always in a fever of excitement. My father was no exception. His nerves spread to us, and Polly and I arrived at the New Theater a good two hours ahead of time. We wanted to be certain not to be late and we also wanted a lot of time to be made-up. The child professionals were to use the dressing room of *The Blue Bird* company, which was playing at the theater. There waiting for us were two men in linen jackets, and a row of wigs.

Nothing smells quite like a wig — that dry, dead scent which has its association only in the world of make-believe. Though my own hair was quite adequate to suggest a child, I seized on a head of henna color with two long braids. Polly chose a blond Dutch cut. Then we sat in front of the brilliantly lit mirrors with towels about our heads and studied our faces hard. We told the men we wanted a great deal of make-up. They obliged. Never was there such a snow-white and rose-red complexion as I achieved. Polly demanded an orange basic to suggest a sunburn and looked like a rather swarthy Hans Brinker.

Tina arrived much later with Mrs. Varesi, who was carrying a valise and a large package. Mrs. Varesi made up Tina's face using hardly any make-up and no mascara on her eyelashes. Tina did not even wear a wig. She wasn't having any fun at all. She hardly spoke to us; she was an actress already living her part.

There was the sound of the orchestra tuning up, and my mother had not yet brought Polly her fruits. Polly did not need these props until the second act, but the agitation of an opening had spread to everyone. The Ox was having trouble with his head and said he could not breathe, much less sing. The beard of one of the Wise Men kept slipping off his chin, and the Virgin was peering through a hole in the curtain and protesting hysterically that her friends had not been given good enough seats.

My father appeared behind the scenes, begged the Star of Bethlehem to keep her eye on his beat and not to drag it so, gave one horrified look at Polly's complexion and mine, and went out to take his place. There was applause, the house lights were dimmed, and the footlights went up.

We sang our way through the first part without mishap, sustained largely by Tina, who became a little dynamo. The value of technique was made clear to me, for Tina seemed truly a little peasant girl dancing with her friends and then awed and humbled by the majesty of the Star. The scene went well, but it was not because of my henna braids: it was the tempo of Tina.

As the lights were lowered again for the second act, my mother finally arrived and handed Polly a small paper bag. "Here it is. You're fine, but what have you done to your face!"

Polly opened the bag. My mother had been seized with one of those fits of economy which we felt sometimes overcame her at the wrong moments. The bag contained one very small cauliflower with a pink slip marked eighteen cents.

"Form in line for the procession of the Star," called the director.

Then Tina appeared. Her father, the grocer, had not neglected her. In her arms she carried a great straw tray, and on it were piled hothouse grapes, bananas, celery, festoons of asparagus, Boston lettuce, and a cornucopia of nuts and raisins. It looked for all the world like a Dean Bon Voyage Basket. Polly was speechless.

The procession proceeded toward the manger. A radiant light fell on the Virgin by the cradle, and the Ox and the Ass, looking through their mouths at my father's baton, sang to us. The three Kings, resplendent in their robes, marched forward.

I presented my doll, and the Virgin indicated that I

place it on the lowest step. The other children in pairs gave their gifts. The last to come forward were Tina and Polly. I suppose that if this scene had truly taken place in medieval times there would have been a miracle. The cauliflower would have turned to gold or blossomed. Instead it seemed to shrink to the size of a tennis ball.

The Virgin had become a little excited over the offerings. She had apparently forgotten the waxen Baby by her side and was accepting the gifts as some sort of personal tribute. In pantomime she showed an increasing surprise and pleasure, climaxed by Tina's great display of fruition. She motioned Tina to come nearer and expressed her admiration for this very expensive present by extending her arms and giving Tina her most brilliant smile. She pointed to her feet as the place of honor and indicated that Tina should place the straw tray there.

Polly waited nervously. Nothing happened. The Virgin ignored her. Then the great chorus began, so Polly determinedly walked up the steps and pushed her cauliflower into the cradle with the Baby. Somehow she knew that He was nearer her own age and would understand. What she did not know was that she had unconsciously righted a scene and made it Christmas again.

Several years later my father decided to revive this opera and give it during the Christmas holidays. He had been to Salzburg, where the pageant form had cast a kind of spell over him. He planned to make this production a much larger one and give it at a new auditorium called the Mecca, which had aisles wide enough for the biggest of processions.

Here my father's imagination ran away with him. When he described a great medieval crowd coursing forward, led and lit by the glow of a star held by an angel, it sounded fine, but we pointed out to him that no star, even with a hundred-watt bulb, would give that amount of light.

"Leave it to me," said my father. "Kaunitz, who lives around the corner on Third Avenue, is a clever electrician. I'll explain to him what I want."

Since I knew the opera, I helped direct the children. A number of schools agreed to furnish the choruses from their pupils, and three chorus masters who were tall asked if they might be the Kings. It gave them a chance to keep an eye on the children and to be part of the show.

Anita, who had come back from Paris that autumn, asserted her independence. She washed her hands of the performance. She was politely interested when plans were discussed, but she refused to have anything to do with it. She had three new hats and other interests.

My father began to have trouble with the star. It seemed the angel would have to carry the battery in her robes, like a kangaroo with its young. He visited his friend on Third Avenue several times but, detecting a skepticism on our part, only told us that he was working it out. Our home filled up again with singers, and rehearsals were on in full force.

The day of the performance, Polly and I rode over in a taxi with my father, who was carrying the star on a wand. It was too long to fit into the cab, so we had to open the windows and lay it sideways. The day was icy, but there was no other way to take it. Suddenly its light began to go on and off in a series of distress signals.

"Look out! You're pressing on the battery!" cried my father.

"I haven't touched it!" I answered. "It's on your lap."

The star shot out another SOS.

"For God's sake, I tell you one of you is pressing a wire. Leave my star alone!"

We knew better than to get into an argument before a performance, but people in the street were beginning to stare. The star went out. My father touched it delicately and it signaled again with greater violence.

"He guaranteed it would give a steady, golden glow," muttered my father. "The damn fool!"

He carefully carried it into the theater and called for the house electrician.

The first half of the performance went well. Great fir trees decorated the corners of the stage and the aisles. The large chorus of children sang with beauty and simplicity; and as the lovely music sounded, a feeling of reverence and Christmas happiness existed between the performers and the audience.

In the intermission Polly and I went around to the greenroom to see my father and tell him how it sounded out front. His face was red and indignant.

"Tell Anita to come here immediately!"

"Anita? She hasn't anything to do with the performance."

"Get her. We haven't much time."

Anita appeared, accompanied by a young violinist, Sam Dushkin, who had only recently returned from Paris and combined excellence of playing with exceptionally polished French manners.

My father asked Sam Dushkin to wait outside; then he turned to Anita and gave her a searching look.

"Yes, you'll do. You're big enough."

"Big enough for what?" asked Anita.

"Get into it quickly. We haven't much time."

"What are you talking about?"

"Jameson, the third chorus master, has telephoned he

has a sore throat. A complete lack of responsibility. He doesn't have to sing a note."

"What have I got to do with him?"

"He's a Wise Man. You'll have to take his place."

"What!"

"You're taller than Gretchen or Polly. You can wear the robes over your dress. Hurry up!"

"I will not," Anita announced, "walk down the aisle of Mecca Auditorium as a Wise Man."

"No one will recognize you," said my father. "You're the black one."

Anita's face turned purple. "I absolutely refuse!"

My father then gave the oldest theatrical battle cry: "But this is a performance!"

"Then you'll have to play it with two Wise Men," replied Anita.

"You'll look like a nice, rather young, colored Santa Claus," urged Polly softly. Anita gave her an icy stare.

My father looked at his watch. "It's a beautiful costume. I borrowed it from the Metropolitan. It's from *Aïda*."

"I don't care," said Anita.

My father now went into a metamorphosis. Though in excellent health, he became the frail old music master deserted by everyone. "You mean you won't help me out when I've worked so hard?"

"No," said Anita.

The make-up man appeared, carrying a lot of dark hair and a pot of black paint. "It's getting late, Mr. Damrosch."

There was the familiar sound of the orchestra tuning up. The feeling of urgency increased. Polly and I left. With Sam Dushkin we walked to the back of the house and waited with the standees to watch the great procession.

First came the Star glowing steady and true. Then the shepherds and the children singing softly as they bore their gifts. There was a roll of drums, the tempo of the orchestra increased, and the three Magi rounded the corner preparing to go down the aisle.

Sam Dushkin looked and unfortunately recognized Balthazar, who was having a little trouble with his robes, which were too long. Sam stepped forward and with gallantry and Old World courtliness offered the outraged King his arm. Balthazar indignantly took it and Polly and I gazed with a strange fascination as they too turned the corner. Sam pressed the unhappy King's dark hand to his lips and left him to march haughtily down the aisle with anything but Christmas love in his black heart. I think some of the audience may have wondered why at this moment there was a salvo of applause from the back of the house.

8

Courage and Convictions

CERTAIN principles are confused in the mind of a child. Grown-up people are busy; but unless issues are properly explained, great walls of misunderstanding can arise. Children are loyal; and if their parents feel deeply about some cause, they will feel deeply also, though often they haven't the faintest idea what it is about.

When I was very little, I felt that there was something wrong about being a Democrat. I didn't know what a Democrat was, where he fitted in — I wasn't even sure he was an American — but I did know he was an outcast. I knew that my mother was the daughter of James G. Blaine, a great Republican, and that that was something to be very proud of. I had heard my mother and my aunt talk over campaigns and elections where his leadership had been challenged. Even when I was very small I knew the bitter feelings that can arise in political life.

One summer day my cousin Walker and I — we were about five years old — were walking through the woods at Bar Harbor. We were considering adventuring on a new path where with luck we might get lost. As we debated this possibility, we saw coming toward us a young man in white flannels — Amos Pinchot. We told him of our problem. He was sympathetic and pointed out a new path that he would take us on some day, and where he promised us we should be well lost. Then he pulled out of his pocket two buttons and pinned them on our chests.

"Wear these and your mothers will do what you ask," he told us.

"Anything?"

"Anything," he promised us.

On each button was the face of an eagle-eyed man with hair that curled over his collar. Underneath the face were some letters, but we did not know how to read.

We wore our buttons hopefully in to lunch, eager to see how soon their magic would begin. My aunt was the first to notice them.

"What have you got on?" she asked.

"Mr. Pinchot gave them to us," I told her proudly.

My aunt started to laugh. "Margaret, look. They're Bryan buttons!"

My mother did not take it so lightly. "Get rid of them immediately!" she cried. "No one can wear a Bryan button in this house. Destroy them!"

Walker and I bolted upstairs to the bathroom, where we disposed of the buttons. Walker was more informed than I. "He's a *Democrat*," he told me.

I had often heard the Democratic Party spoken of with great disapproval. To me a party meant ice cream and chocolate cake, so I assumed from the gloomy reports that when the Democrats gave their parties they were always failures. I often wondered what went wrong. Did the guests not arrive, or was it like so many parties — not quite so much fun as one had expected? The Republican parties, I gathered, were great successes. Everyone came.

When I grew a little older and did begin faintly to understand that this all referred to a political structure, the first picture was so engraved on my mind that when the parties were referred to, I continued to see a lace cloth and candies and the ever-present threat that something was going to spoil the occasion. And to this day I cannot rid myself of that first impression. My mother imbued us with so strong a feeling of loyalty to the Republican Party that when I have deviated and voted the Democratic ticket, I have done so with a sense of wrong toward her, and I am still nervous about telling her.

At the last election, I confessed to her that I was going to vote for President Roosevelt. My mother told me to do what I thought was right. This gesture on her part, which was a big gesture, only increased my old sense of guilt; and as I stood in the polling booth, the same picture rose to my eyes again, of the tables covered with snappers and cakes, and I was sitting at the table where something might go wrong. I wasn't at my mother's party.

My mother told us not to talk about Catholics at table. I am not sure that it was as direct as that, but if the word "Catholic" came up in conversation she would say, "Hush," and look at the pantry door. We frequently had nice Irish maids and my mother must have been afraid that something carelessly said might hurt their feelings. Actually I do not think any of us would conceivably have made an attack on the Church, because, except for a little colorful reading on the Inquisition and some history of the Holy Roman Empire ("Give its boundaries"), we were completely ignorant about Catholicism. But because of the "Hush" and the look at the pantry, I became convinced that there was something very wrong and quite unmentionable about being a Catholic.

If my father suddenly sang "The Pope, He Leads a Jolly Life," I was in a panic. The fact that the current Lizzie or Norah smiled broadly did not matter. My father was doing something dangerous, and the Pope — well, almost like the Holy Ghost — should never, never be mentioned.

Alice told me she had a friend at school who was a "you know what."

"She goes," said Alice, letting her voice sink, "to Confessional."

"What does she confess?" I whispered.

"Her Sins!" said Alice.

I was back in a novel of Sir Walter Scott.

"Point her out to me," I begged. "I just want to look at her."

One day I took my courage in my hands and went alone on a weekday to a Catholic Church. I was as furtive as any criminal. I had prepared a speech if I was challenged at the door. I was going to say, "Sure, I'm waiting for me aunt, Lizzie Dougherty."

I felt I could make it right with Lizzie later. My father had taken me to a performance of *Manon*, so I suppose I expected to see a number of ladies in satin evening dresses, with black veils over their heads, adoringly following an abbé as they sang: —

> *Quelle éloquence!*
> *L'admirable orateur!*
> *Quelle abondance!*
> *Le grand prédicateur! . . .*

C'est lui, c'est l'abbé Des Grieux,
Voyez comme il baisse les yeux!

No one spoke to me. I sat down in a pew fearful of making a flagrant mistake which would unmask me. Then I knelt and looked about. A woman lit a candle by an altar and placed it with some other candles. Then she sank to her knees and prayed. A man with two children sat quietly in another pew. A couple were walking up one of the side aisles looking at the religious paintings. A priest followed by two little boys passed in front of the altar, genuflected, and went through a door. I was left alone, to think, to watch. I found I liked it.

This visit weighed on my conscience like going to a matinee on a schoolday and I finally told my mother. She received the news calmly.

"I used to go to the services when I lived at the convent," she told me.

"When you lived *where!*" I exclaimed.

"When I was at the Sacré-Coeur at school," said my mother.

My mother then told me of the winter she had spent at the Sacred Heart Convent in Paris. This turned my world upside down. My mother had lived in a convent. What was more, she made it sound human and not strange at all. Why then was there such a conspiracy of silence when the word "Catholic" was mentioned?

Another "Hush" was given if anyone spoke of a summer plan, particularly if there was a hint of a trip to Europe involved. Apparently at the mention of a foreign country, a walkout strike might occur on the other side of the pantry door. My mother and father would start talking to each other in rapid French concerning *"Londres pour deux semaines,"* but I used to wonder if a smart maid didn't catch on even more quickly than I did as to what was up.

It is hard to keep secrets in a big family. Children are unconscious detectives and have their own methods of getting information. One great help to my sisters and me was the registers that went like an internal communication service through the house. When they were opened they blew out medium or cold air, according to the floor, some coal dust, and human sounds.

My mother's register was directly below Alice's and mine and we learned a great deal of what she and my father were up to, particularly when we dried our hair. Before the days of movie stars, hair was not washed every twenty-four hours. It was washed — hard — at rare intervals by Minnie, with ammonia and tar soap. Then we dried it by the register, where a little coal dust was added to it again, and we listened to my parents. January was the best month for getting the news. The house was always freezing and everyone opened every register. The sounds were mingled and it took a certain ingenuity to separate the reports accurately. Alice and I would crouch on the floor with towels over our shoulders and listen.

"Will ye kindly use the knife for the butter and keep your big spoon do re me fa sol why don't you meet me in Denver for the California tour the children will be all right for a few play B flat for God's sake Anita you took the cream I saw you Alma Gluck will be soloist and we'll have a jolly time."

So my mother was going to join my father on the orchestra tour. This was the big news. We listened to it with mingled feelings. It would mean more freedom for us, but it would also mean, we knew from experience, that the household would temporarily fall to pieces.

When my mother left on these trips, life continued normally for about five days. But Minnie, a suspicious dragon, was waiting, as we all were, for the crack-up. The first warning came when our ring was not answered for a long time and the front door was finally opened by the cook in a pink peekaboo blouse. We apologized because she had been put to this trouble, and she answered that she did not know where Jenny was. Jenny appeared late to serve supper, and her head was covered with curls.

That night the "cousins" arrived. The cousins were

all young men of about twenty-three, handsome and assured, and were waiting in the areaway. The next night they were inside the kitchen and giving a dance. The house shook from the pounding of feet; wild shrieks, laughter, and the sound of an accordion came up registers and hallways. Minnie, walking up and down like a Cassandra in an apron, cried out warnings on the Irish, my parents, America, and said she would call the police. But the police were cousins. The next morning we did nothing. At supper whipped cream appeared on the cocoa as a reward for keeping our mouths shut, and for two days everything was calm again. Then there was another party; card games, prizes, a reel, and a late supper.

As the time drew near for my mother's return, a mysterious change took place. The floors were waxed, my mother's curtains were washed, and Jenny told us how lonesome and silent the house had seemed without "your dear mother attending to things." It was as though we had dreamed about the gaieties. And when my mother appeared, tired from a long continental trip, we couldn't meet her with bad news. We kept to our whipped-cream agreement of saying nothing.

My mother in terms of today was tough on her household, and the word "appeasement" had not yet been invented. Maids either left in a series of quick turnovers or stayed for many years. My mother was not only clear-cut on what she wanted, but she expected the work to be done in what she called "a cheerful spirit." With what seems to me now incredible courage, she would inform a heavily breathing cook, who had climbed three flights of stairs to hear the good news, that my father had invited sixteen people to a late supper and it must be hot because my father loathed cold food. I would listen, trembling, to the dialogue.

"Sure, Mrs. Damrosch, that stove won't heat right and it's my Thursday night off."

"Norah," said my mother, "the stove has never had anything done to it for twenty years. I will try to give you another night out if I can arrange it, later in the month. But smile, Norah, take that frown off your face!" And unbelievable as it sounds, Norah produced a watery smile and tottered down again quite cheerfully to her basement kitchen.

The maids all respected my mother for her fairness and knew that she would go to endless trouble if they were sick or in difficulties. But what they admired her for was her courage. My mother had moral courage but she possessed what I think is the rarer trait, great physical bravery.

Many children seem to have very beautiful early impressions of their mother — a *berceuse*, a figure in white picking roses. A first memory of my mother was seeing her in the dead center of a dogfight trying to separate a bulldog's jaws from a Scotch terrier's throat. The sounds were hideous, a high, hysteric yelping, as my mother whirled both dogs around several feet off the ground, occasionally stopping to put her fist into the bulldog's mouth in an effort to pry it wider open.

Over the years we had many dogs and there were many fights. At one time we kept a hose permanently coiled and ready for an eternal feud that went on between a police dog and a Scottie. As the hair on Kebo, the police dog, began to rise, we started the water trickling through the nozzle, which was turned on to full power only when Locky appeared, walking stiff-legged and muttering to himself.

Once a cacophony of sounds broke out beyond the music room where my father was playing the piano. He stopped abruptly. "Get your mother!" he shouted. "She likes dogfights!"

It took my mother, whose wrist carried the imprint of several teeth, a full week to forgive him.

The dogs loved my mother for this fearlessness, and when one of them was badly hurt, he would limp to her knowing she would pick him up in her arms no matter how much he was bleeding. And when the end drew near for some old friend, my mother would put him away herself, alone in the stable, holding his paw till the last.

My sisters and I went through a period of great tenderheartedness for animals, which reached the last stages of morbidity. Polly decided that she knew how it felt to be a horse. She took the checkreins off all horses that she saw in the village and hid or stole the whips. A drive with Polly was a slow affair. There were frequent stops to give the horse water, to brush the bluebottles off him, to let him eat some grass because he must be hungry; and when a little hill appeared, Polly would force her passenger to get out with her and walk beside the horse so that he wouldn't get tired.

I was worried about the fate of flies. Instead of killing them, I tried to let them out through the screen door so that they could rejoin their families. I had to shepherd them as a flock through two rooms, and the flies would not stay in a compact group. I destroyed flypaper as soon as it appeared because the death buzz was so agonizing. I tried to argue this out with my mother, winding up with the question: —

"How would you like to be a fly?"

"Gammon!" said my mother.

At this time cars were not common, and country homes could be lonely places at dusk. For many years at our country home on Lake Champlain we had only oil lamps and candles, and it was not possible to snap on lights over doorways or along passages. We lit lamps in the rooms that we were using, and carried candles elsewhere.

One twilight a tramp came through the grounds and wandered up to the back door. Polly and I saw him from an upper window and our hearts welled over for this poor, shabby man. Norah looked at his red eyes and blue chin, got a whiff of his breath, and immediately as a matter of course called for my mother. Norah was younger than my mother and about seventy-five pounds heavier.

When my mother appeared, the tramp began to tell her in a low, whining voice that his feet hurt, that he was out of work, sleeping God knows where —

"Take off your hat when you are speaking to a lady!" commanded my mother.

Startled, the tramp pulled off his cap.

"You can't get work?" asked my mother.

"It's food I need to get my strength back, and a bed, and a little money for shoes — "

"You may split that wood into kindling," announced my mother, "and when it's done I'll give you thirty-five cents." My mother, for some unknown reason, always made her financial arrangements in odd figures.

The last thing the tramp wanted was work. He wanted a couple of dollars and with no trouble to himself. He then made a big mistake. An ugly light came into his eye and he started to threaten my mother.

"It's the rich like you in your fine homes that will deny a poor man a crust. I won't be treated like a dog. I want a dollar and you'd better get it quick!"

My mother's face turned the color of claret.

"I am going to stand here and count to ten, and if you are not off my property by the last count, I'll throw you off the place myself!"

The tramp looked at my mother. My mother looked back at him fiercely. It was growing darker. Norah had slunk inside the door, while Polly and I from our window watched with absorbed interest. We didn't know whom we wanted to win.

"One — two — three — " began my mother.

The tramp stood his ground.

"Four — five — " my mother continued at the same pace. "Six — seven — "

By eight the tramp wavered and at nine he was shambling down the road muttering to himself.

"Sure, you're the fighting cock!" exclaimed Norah admiringly.

"That poor, hungry man," Polly and I cried out.

"How could you be so mean and scare him so!"

"Double gammon," said my mother.

Once a fracas took place which assumed considerable proportions. It was in the city on election day, and our windows were filled with campaign posters. A man who must have started the morning with a good many drinks came weaving down the street, saw the posters in our windows, and decided that this was his polling booth. Just as he was about to enter the house, my mother opened the door prepared to go out.

"What do you want?" asked my mother.

The man did not answer but tried to push past her so that he could cast his vote quickly. My mother jumped in front of him and barred the entrance.

"You can't come in here like this!" she cried.

"Ish my right," said the man thickly, "my inalienable right."

"Get out!" cried my mother.

The man gave a big shove. "Ish my right," he repeated. "Ish inalienable. I'm coming in."

My mother tried to throw him back again but he was bigger than she, and she saw that she needed help.

"Children," she shouted, "there's a man out here who wants to kill your father!"

I do not know what made her reach this conclusion

so rapidly, but she was excited and had apparently convinced herself that this must be his intention.

Two of us ran out and saw my mother and a murderer locked in a struggle in the entranceway. We jumped beside her and tried to push him down the stone steps so that he would fall on his head backwards. The man was now aroused. The spirit of the Constitution flamed up in him, and come hell or high water, he was determined to get in and cast his vote.

"I'm an American shitizen. I'm the only one that's got the right to go in there."

"How dare you!" exclaimed my mother.

"You haven't got the franchishe!" And he gave her a baleful but triumphant look.

This was too much for my mother. Not only was this man an assassin but he was an antisuffragist.

"You'll get the electric chair for this," she told him briefly.

At this moment my father came up the street and saw his wife and two of his daughters battling on the stoop with a stranger whose hat had been knocked off and whose tie was on backwards.

"Stay away, Walter!" screamed my mother. "He wants to kill you!"

My father was infuriated — not against the man, but because my mother assumed that he needed her protection and couldn't fight for himself. He came rushing up the steps to join in but was still sufficiently cool to tell one of us to run to the election booth at the corner and get a policeman.

It took a good deal of explaining when the policeman came pounding down the block to drag the man away. Weakly my mother sat down on the top step.

"But, Margaret," protested my father, "why didn't you listen to his story and find out what he wanted?"

"There wasn't time. I thought he was going to shoot you."

"He was going to vote, probably the Republican ticket, and now they've taken him off and you've lost that vote for your side!"

My mother looked more stricken than if he'd killed my father.

"He was a Democrat," we comforted her.

"Then I did right," said my mother.

9

Reading and Writing

THAT reading could be a joy and a resource came to me as a glad surprise when I was given the *Dotty Dimple* and the *Five Little Peppers* books. It is difficult to analyze why a certain series becomes so popular with a child, but the ingredients that make for this success seem to be a large family, so that one can identify oneself with a character one's own age, a day-by-day account of the characters, and great dullness. There is a fascination about dullness. It immediately eliminates competition.

Dotty was the youngest member of the Parlin family. She had two older sisters, Prudy and Susy, and her parents, Mr. and Mrs. Parlin. There were also Aunt Madge, who visited them for many months, Mrs. Read, their Quaker grandmother, a mischievous little cousin who lisped, called Flaxie Frizzle, and Cousin Horace.

The sisters dressed in the morning, they went to school, they came home, they ate their meals, they played a little, they went to bed. It was as absorbing as an account of the Borgias. I loved the Parlins. I worried over their troubles and rejoiced in their happiness. I secretly became Prudy. My only fear was that the books would end, but year after year Sophie May continued to play Boswell to this blameless family.

Mrs. Parlin was very unlike my own mother. She wore an apron and was always ready with a cookie and a bit of advice. When Prudy told her "white lie," the climax of many chapters, Mrs. Parlin resorted to tears and an apple. The Parlin girls also wore aprons and bonnets and tippets. They had little duties to perform, like sweeping the hearth or fetching father his slippers. I would have gladly brought my father his slippers, but he always changed his shoes in his own room and seemed to need no help.

When an older person addressed the girls, they answered, "Yes'm" or "No'm."

"Thee must think before thee speaks, little Prudy," said Grandmother Read.

"Yes'm," answered Prudy earnestly.

Aunt Madge, who was pretty, sewed very well. The sisters would sit in her bedroom and would make the most remarkable variety of interesting things under the direction of "her nimble fingers." Now I had an Aunt H. who was also very pretty. But she did not wear an apron. We never sat with her through the long afternoons while "her needle flashed in and out of the soft muslin." We often went into her room. But it was to examine all the silver brushes and bottles she had on the dressing table, or to try on her hats.

The Five Little Peppers were much poorer than the Parlins. They lived in a little brown house and their mother was a widow. Mrs. Pepper was really up against it. Often there was no coal, the furniture was broken, and the lack of clothing was a serious problem. But such was the indomitable spirit of Mrs. Pepper that the little brown house was always full of hope.

Polly, the oldest girl, was the heroine of the series. She had brown hair which curled a little, and brown eyes, and she helped "Mamsie," as the children called their mother, see the family through their troubles. Mamsie was not so gentle as Mrs. Parlin. It seemed to me she almost preferred the hard way.

"Oh, I wish," said Joey discontentedly, pushing back his bowl of mush and molasses, "we could have something new to eat."

"Better be glad you've got that, Joey," said Mrs. Pepper, taking another cold potato and sprinkling a little salt on it.

In the town where the Peppers lived was a rich old man called Mr. King, who had a son Jasper just two years older than Polly. Jasper began to sneak away from his home full of rugs and conservatories and a grand piano, and go to the little brown house.

Well, you can imagine what happened. Mr. King was indignant and wanted the Peppers thrown out of the town. Little Phronsie Pepper, a girl of about five, went to see Mr. King and told him exactly how she felt. And as Jasper's health had improved — he was a delicate boy — Mr. King swallowed his pride and called on Mamsie. Then, after considering the matter very briefly, Mr. King invited Mamsie and the five children to come and live with him in his carpeted home, and asked Mamsie to become his housekeeper. That he wanted her for this particular role was surprising, for Mrs. Pepper's ideas of food were, to say the least, austere. But Mamsie always seemed to inspire confidence in older men. Several years later she married Dr. Fisher, a widower with gleaming spectacles, who adored the way she cooked.

As Polly grew older, I began to suspect that Jasper was falling in love with her. There was only a hint here, a hint there, but if one studied the passages very carefully, it was fair to conclude that something was happening. I had never read a love scene. Finally, in the sixth volume, the twenty-second chapter, I came to it. Polly had been away in the city as a music teacher and had just returned home.

Polly, in a soft white gown, sat on a low seat by Mother Fisher's side, her head in Mamsie's lap. It was after dinner and the gas was turned low.

"Mamsie," said Polly, and she threw one hand over her head to clasp Mother Fisher's strong fingers closer, "it's so good to be home — oh! you can't think how I wanted you."

Just then somebody looked into Mother Fisher's bedroom.

"Oh! beg pardon," said Jasper, as he saw them. But there was so much longing in the voice that Polly called out, "Oh! Come, Jasper. May he, Mamsie?"

"Yes," said Mrs. Fisher, "come in, Jasper," and made room for him to sit down by her side.

"Now isn't this nice!" breathed Polly, lifting her head out of her mother's lap to look at him on Mamsie's other side.

"I want to tell you something," began Jasper quietly to Mrs. Fisher, " — and to you too, Polly. Mrs. Fisher — may I speak?" He leaned over and looked into the black eyes above Polly's shining brown hair.

"Yes," said Mother Fisher as quietly.

"Polly," said Jasper, "look at me, do, dear!"

Polly lifted her brown eyes quietly. "Why, Jasper?"

He put out his hand and Polly instinctively laid her own

warm palm within it. "Do you think you could love me — I've loved you ever since the Little Brown House days, dear!"

"Oh, Jasper!" Polly cried, with a glad ring in her voice, "how good you are," and she clung to his hand across Mamsie's lap.

"Will you, Polly?" cried Jasper, holding her hand so tight that she winced a bit, "tell me quickly, dear."

"Will I what?" asked Polly wonderingly.

"Love me, Polly."

"Oh! I do — I do," she cried, "you know it, Jasper. I love you with all my heart."

"Polly, will you marry me? Tell her, Mrs. Fisher, do, and make her understand," begged Jasper, turning to Mother Fisher imploringly.

"Polly, child," said Mamsie, putting both arms around her, careful not to disturb Jasper's hand over Polly's, "Jasper wants you to be his wife — do you love him enough for that?"

Polly, not taking her brown eyes from Jasper's face, laid her other hand upon his. "I love him enough," she said, "for that; oh, Jasper!" . . .

"I always wanted to call you Mamsie," said Jasper looking into Mrs. Fisher's face, "and now I can!"

I was outraged. Was that the way a proposal was made? Was this romance? Dimly I felt that here art was not imitating nature. It was not true. I turned from the Peppers. I did not like them,

That same sense of fury came to me again a year or two later. But this time I had to believe it, for it was a great book — *Little Women*. I was reading about real, unpredictable people and everything seemed right, and then I came to one of the shortest proposals in literature, yet one of the most beautiful, but it was between the wrong pair.

Amy and Laurie were on the Lake of Geneva and Amy remarked that they rowed well together.

"So well, that I wish we might always pull together. Will you, Amy?" — very tenderly.

"Yes, Laurie." — Very low.

Why did Laurie have to choose the blond Amy? I never liked her. Why did he not win Jo, who was the grand character of them all? My resentment against Louisa Alcott on this score has never died.

One cannot read without sooner or later wanting to try to write oneself, and fortunately there was a door wide open to young authors — the *St. Nicholas Magazine*.

The first part of the *St. Nicholas* was an honest-to-goodness magazine. There were short stories, articles, poems, pictures, and two serials. For many years Ralph Henry Barbour was its Trollope. He never stopped writing. Hardly had the last word appeared in *The*

New Boy at Hilltop when *Tom, Dick and Harriet* began. On the heels of *Harry's Island* came *Captain Chub* and *The Magic Foot-ball*. Though the books were for boys, the girls read them. They were very exciting. A fine fellow was accused of cheating and took the blame so that it would not fall on his best friend, who was also under suspicion, and it was not until nearly the last chapter that the whole matter was cleared up and a very unpleasant boy was found to be the guilty one.

Frances Hodgson Burnett wrote *Racketty-Packetty House* for *St. Nicholas*. George Madden Martin wrote *Emmy Lou* and *Abbie Ann*. Alice Hegan Rice frequently contributed. The best writers were there. But the serial system was tantalizing and the words "To be continued" an agony. It was too long to wait a whole month to see what happened.

This torture was as nothing to the anticipation of a contributor to the St. Nicholas League. There were about eight pages of competitions in the back of the magazine. They were in Verse, Prose, Drawing, Photography, Puzzle Making, and Puzzle Answers. There were stern rules for the contestants. One was allowed to write on only one side of the paper, and the writing must be in ink. The contribution had to be in by a certain date. Parents or teachers countersigned the paper, attesting that they were convinced beyond doubt that the contribution had not been copied. But if one carefully lived up to all the rules, the possibilities of reward were enormous.

One could win a gold or silver badge. One could be on the Roll of Honor. At one time there were cash prizes of five dollars. But best of all there was one's own worked-over poem or story actually in print, like a book, under one's own *printed* name.

The subjects were varied. The artists drew "A Heading for March" or "My Favorite Nook." The photographers took pictures of "A Hot Day," "A Busy Street," or "An Animal Friend." They were all snapped by Brownie Jr. Kodaks.

The poets and prose writers were the most persistently regular contributors. They drew the deepest on their own inspiration and worked the hardest. A silver badge for a poem meant much more than a silver badge for a snapshot. It was the real thing. The poets wrote verses on "The Land of Romance," "The Star," "A Patriot," and "Friendship." A girl called E. Vincent Millay won badge after badge. Two boys, S. V. Benét and Robert Hillyer, did exceptionally well.

In the prose articles the authors really let themselves go and ran the whole gamut of experience. "A Historic Christmas" or "A Family Tradition" produced fairly orthodox pieces. The editors must have had in mind the training of future writers for the *Reader's Digest* when they asked for articles on "What Experience in My Life Has Been of the Greatest Help to Me." But sometimes the subjects were too popular and the badges had to be given right and left. This occurred when the authors were asked to give an account of "Lost in a Storm."

It seemed as though every reader of the *St. Nicholas* had had this dreadful experience. Hundreds of harrowing stories poured in. America was full of children huddled under pine trees, deserted in ravines, nearly struck again and again by bolts of lightning, hanging desperately to overturned canoes, lost and lost again, and yet miraculously saved and able to describe their terrible adventures.

Rachel Field was a heavy contributor. She made many of the other authors jealous. They felt she must be showing off, she used such long words. A puzzle extremely difficult to solve was sent in by a boy named Hamilton Fish Armstrong. It was called "A Roman Zigzag." For this he received a badge.

There was still one further opportunity for writing, and that was to The Letter Box. Boys and girls from all over the world wrote in, describing their foreign homes and their glad excitement when the *St. Nicholas* arrived by camel or sled. Foreign children who were also members of the League sent greetings to the American members.

YALTA, CRIMEA, RUSSIA

DEAR ST. NICHOLAS: —

I seldom see letters from Russia so I thought I would write you one. I am a pupil of the Imperial Lyceum at St. Petersburg. I am staying for my health in the Crimea, a few versts from Sevastopol. The railway goes no further than Sevastopol.

The Emperor has a palace called Livadia, about 2 versts from Yalta; almost every day we see some of the imperial family driving about. Yesterday there was a grand bazaar at which were present all the imperial family. The Empress and the four Grand Duchesses, her daughters, presided at the stalls.

My eldest sister who is now married to the Russian naval attaché in Washington took you when she was a girl. I am taking you for the third year and I especially like the serial, "The Runaway."

I am your very interested reader.

VLADIMIR RIMSKY-KORSAKOFF (age 14)

TOKIO, JAPAN

DEAR ST. NICHOLAS: —

For a few months I have been getting you sent by a grown-up friend of mine. I have been your lover since I had you first given by him. . . . I was sorry that I had no father, as he, who was an officer, fell in the Russo-Japanese

War; but happy now as I have found a good friend in you. . . .

I am teaching English to myself by helps of some books. It seems to me a rather hard task to master certain language thoroughly. But I shall fight and conquer all the difficulties and I shall gain your prize. I wish to contribute you proses, in which I tell you something about Japan. . . . Japan is the romantic realm of the world; her national idea, sceneries, and what belongs to Japan is all romantic. I dare say, I am myself a romantic boy.

I always wish that many American boys could correspond with us the Japanese, as I believe that the correspondence would, no doubt, produce an appreciable friendship. . . . That friendship might be called "Little Jap-American Alliance." . . .

With best wishes, I am

Your loving reader in Japan,

PENTARROW MOCHIZUKI

Editorial comment:—

Here is a very interesting and highly creditable letter from a "romantic" boy-reader of this magazine, in faraway Japan. His resolve to master the difficult English language, and his evident friendly feeling for America are heartily to be commended.

It must have rained a great deal in the days of *St. Nicholas*. I do not wish to pass a moral judgment on the virtue of rain, but there is no doubt that when the heavens opened and one was shut in the house, it was up to one's own ingenuity to provide amusement.

There was making fudge. It took about forty minutes, and no one ever had sufficient patience to let it harden enough. The *St. Nicholas* gave a great deal of advice on fudge.

There was cutting out and pasting. We all had big scrapbooks which were called houses. We cut out of magazines pictures of elegant sofas and chairs and pasted them in the rooms. The kitchen was full of hardware advertisements, the garden a mass of seed-catalogue suggestions.

We dressed up. We took what we dared of my mother's dresses and hats and then we either played store or called on each other, talking in high-pitched and cultured voices which we had never heard used by any adult. As we poured water out of a china teapot into little cups, we crooked our fingers.

Polly always took the name of Madame Delton. Wearing a tall turban and a spotted veil, she would tell us how things were going in the Delton ménage and we in turn would describe our own affairs. The point of the tea party was of course to do all the talking and keep the conversation on oneself. Then Polly would skillfully begin to hog the subject. She would throw out dark hints about Mr. Delton. He had not been around lately. She thought he might be in prison. It was almost discourteous not to ask what Mr. Delton had done. Polly seized her opportunity.

"The Inspector came to see me last night."

Our own accounts of shopping expeditions and children's diseases paled. Mr. Delton was not the best of husbands. He was in fact quite awful. But he had that rare quality of interest. No matter what new evil he dreamt up to inflict on the unfortunate Madame Delton, we grudgingly but inevitably wanted to hear the whole story.

The monsoons must have continued, for finally the *St. Nicholas* decided to do something about it. The editors ran a group of rainy-day suggestions for mothers and nurses. This was a great mistake. One of these was headed "How to Make a Suspension Bridge out of Old Spools," and was full of diagrams with dotted lines. Another described "Useful Ornaments for the Home Made of Colored String." No household had enough old spools or colored string. No nurses, much less mothers, wanted to be bothered. The projects were never finished. They were in fact impossible. The *St. Nicholas* decided to give up about the weather.

And they were right. These ideas were not really

needed. When all the painting and pasting and dressing up was over, children turned to the bookshelves and hauled out the old red volumes of *St. Nick* of the eighties. Lying on their stomachs they turned the pages and were absorbed in the children of another day; those remote children who wore such different clothes, who had never seen an automobile, who studied by lamp instead of gas light. How strange not to have known of all the exciting things that were ahead of them. Those early children of *St. Nicholas*, so old-fashioned, so different, one could almost pity them. And yet in all the pictures they were laughing, too.

Then, as the rain fell against the windows, children went into a strange, fantastic dream called the future. It was difficult to imagine, but it seemed that there would be a time when one would be grown-up oneself — say twenty years old, or maybe even thirty. Other children then would appear with new ways of doing things. It was not the new children that were so interesting: it was the thought of oneself as different. The dream went into materialistic channels — oneself with an automobile, oneself wearing clothes of one's own choice.

People said the world changed. But it didn't seem likely that much would happen. As one looked at the old books, there had been wars — the Civil War and

Teddy Roosevelt's Rough Riders in the Spanish War. There wouldn't be anything so exciting as that again. That was in history. No, the world seemed pretty well set. The changes would be in that eternally absorbing subject, oneself.

(*10*)

Unfinished Business

My PARENTS felt that our summer holidays were too long. It was disintegrating to lie fallow for four months. In the summer, children could learn — and learn thoroughly — all those things that schools claimed there was no time for. Languages, music and other arts, great literature — there was no limit to how the time could be applied. Even if one could give to it only a couple of hours a day, one could really learn French or get Sir Walter Scott's whole set under one's belt if the work was done regularly. Spring after spring my mother and father hopefully planned, and summer after summer my sisters and I successfully thwarted their efforts.

There were various reasons for these dreadful failures. In the first place the summer months were of such uneven length: June and July were normal, but August went by in a week, and September was over before it began. Our summer holiday seemed to us about two months long, with a little extra time at the end.

One or the other of us often had a disagreeable letter from school, suggesting that we work off a condition in Latin, or redo some algebra against an examination in the autumn. These assignments, though not on the surface so stimulating as something my father had up his sleeve, had the urgency of reality. There was an old wives' tale that children studied for the love of knowledge. At this time we worked only for marks.

But one important reason for these disappointments in living the higher life was that my parents became bored with it all. The work demanded a certain persistence on their part — always met with stubborn resistance by their daughters — and their efforts never lasted long enough to achieve the desired goal.

To announce that at breakfast everyone would speak German ought to be an easy way to make us conversationally fluent. But after a couple of mornings my mother, who did not speak German, found she did not like being inarticulate. She would find something in the papers that interested her and want to discuss it with my father — and who were we to remind them that we were eating in another tongue.

Though my sisters and I did not want to learn anything that was chosen for us, we had of course ambitions. Lying in a hammock with one's eyes fixed on a floating cloud, it was fun to dream of being beautiful and famous, and the more vaporous or vaulting the dream, the more possible did its fulfillment seem. We understood too much about music to feel that careers lay ahead for us there. We knew the work; we knew how good you had to be. We had professional standards. But to be a great actress or writer was conceivable and probable.

Secretly we attempted creations in various forms. We indulged in that unparalleled joy of "starting things." On one bedroom door or another a sign would appear: "Keep Out. No One Must Enter on Pain of Death." We had notebooks with locks and keys. On the first page of Polly's book was written: —

Private.   Secret.
This Means *You*, Gretchen!

My father decided we should read all of Shakespeare aloud, each taking a part. When he realized how many copies of how many plays this would necessitate, he reduced the plan. We were to start with *Julius Caesar*, and he ordered five paper books.

I think he was a little startled when he looked over the cast. He remembered *Caesar* as including some good rousing speeches between Antony and Brutus. He had forgotten that there were some thirty-two other characters, besides senators, citizens, guards, and attendants. It seemed almost impossible to divide these all up. My father, however, decided to be Brutus. We tossed for who should read Antony, and second place went to Caesar. The other parts were to be read around in rotation.

To emphasize the seriousness of the reading, my father decided it was to take place indoors. The dogs were banished outside and lay in an unhappy group just beyond the screen door. We sat in an uneasy circle around my father as he announced: "Act One. Scene One. Rome. A street."

The curtain rose and my father opened as Flavius, in a ringing voice. Alice as Marullus, and I as the Carpenter, jumped in with equal loudness. Polly rotated into the Cobbler and decided to play him as a cracked old man.

" 'But what trade art thou? Answer me directly,' " demanded Alice.

" 'A trade, sir, that I hope I may use with a safe conscience; which is, indeed, sir, a mender of bad soles,' " responded Polly.

" 'What trade, thou knave? Thou naughty knave, what trade?' " my father shouted.

" 'Nay,' " answered Polly, sinking her voice into a

senile whisper, " 'I beseech you, sir, be not out with me; yet, if you be out, sir, I can mend you.' "

The rest of us broke out into wild laughter, and there was a sympathetic thumping of tails from the porch.

"You must be serious," exclaimed my father.

"But it's supposed to be funny."

"Not that funny," said my father, but we continued convulsed with our own interpretations.

Now Shakespeare is often obscure — it would seem at times meaningless. I read: —

> Forget not, in your speed, Antonius,
> To touch Calphurnia; for our elders say,
> The barren, touched in this holy chase,
> Shake off their sterile curse.

"I don't understand that at all. What's it about?"

"It's perfectly simple," said my father, and he studied the passage. "Never mind what it means. It's the spirit we're after." He glanced ahead. "Ah, good. Here comes the Soothsayer. I'll act him."

He sprang to the piano and played some minor chords as he announced in a sepulchral voice: " 'Beware the ides of March.' "

My father had invited my mother to listen to the play, but she refused. She never liked being read aloud to. If my father found a poem that pleased him or one of Finley Peter Dunne's Dooley articles that amused him, he wanted to read it immediately, with dialect, and he did it extremely well. But he needed an audience, and my mother was often the most convenient ear.

"Sit down, Margaret, and listen to this. You'll enjoy it."

My mother would sit for about a minute listening, but then a strange restlessness would seize her. First she would straighten a vase of flowers on the mantel, then tweak the window shades to make them even, and finally walk about swatting flies with a newspaper. My father seemed to find this distracting.

"You're not listening. Sit down."

"I am listening. It's very good. Go on." And my mother would sink to a chair again but start picking burrs out of the dog's hair.

It has been said that in happy marriages husbands and wives often grow to look like each other and eventually evolve a common character. This has not been the case with my father and mother. Over the years their personalities have met, head on, and I have never seen that either one made the slightest dent on the other's character. But what surprised their daughters was that the differences which we recognized in them, and certain storm signals which most families perceive only too quickly when they begin wigwagging on the horizon, always astonished my mother and father.

As children we knew that my mother hated surprises and that my father liked them; that my mother loved picnics and being lost in the woods in the rain and that such things disturbed my father; that he liked certain kinds of European food which my mother would not touch. And yet year after year my father hopefully surprised my mother, my mother tramped my father over mountains with only a sandwich and no path map, and he continued to urge on her food that she would not eat.

Neither ever gave up in trying to change the other and they were continuously thunderstruck at their differences. But perhaps the deeper truth, which we were too young to understand, lay in the fact that neither one enjoyed anything very much unless the other shared it; and if my father wanted to read something aloud, and in the middle of it my mother decided to mow the lawn, my father still found her his best and favorite audience.

My mother's efforts with summer work were a little more successful than my father's because they were not so grandiose. She gave us the choice on Sundays of going to church or having a Bible lesson at home. We learned a psalm, but then we learned anything else that seemed to her important. We memorized among other things the second verse of "The Star-Spangled Banner," and Taft's cabinet.

My mother had bought a great many towels which had no monograms and we marked them with a cross-stitched "D" during the Sunday mornings. The cross-stitch book had some designs of coats of arms, and during the summer the *D*'s became surrounded with heraldic standards. Alice, who was the most ambitious, stitched on Turkish towels the emblems of the Houses of Warwick and Hastings and, tracing her designs from an old book, put the rampant lion of Fraunceys over the washrags.

"Who is Secretary of State?" asked my mother.

"Philander C. Knox."

"Secretary of War?"

"Jacob M. Dickinson."

"Secretary of the Navy?"

"George von L. Meyer. Pass over the blue thread for azure on the garter of Beaufort."

"Secretary of Commerce and Labor?"

"Charles Nagel. Now can we go swimming? It's twelve o'clock."

"Not yet. Attorney General, Postmaster General, Secretary of the Interior."

"George W. Wickersham, Frank H. Hitchcock, Richard A. Ballinger."

We started toward the lake.

"You've forgotten the Treasury," my mother called after us.

"Franklin MacVeagh!" we shouted back. The Bible lesson was over.

Another effort of my mother was to improve the tone of conversation at table. If members of a family see each other constantly at meals, talk is likely to degenerate into personalities often emphasized by swift kicks under the table. We were requested to make no remarks about each other's physical or spiritual shortcomings. This reduced us to chitchat about our friends and neighbors, and children quite as much as grownups find the odd or eccentric more interesting to analyze than the nobler traits of their fellows.

None of us liked Dr. Colton, the local doctor. He didn't stay a doctor. He was quite a lady's man, and he also played a rather feverish game of tennis. We did not approve of seeing him one day in a white coat, advising something disagreeable, and the next day in a turtleneck sweater, making what we felt was a fool of himself on the court by serving a very easy ball to the ladies and then apologizing as though it had been an ace. He was for us always a good subject of conversation and we vied with each other in pointing out his weaknesses.

"Everyone around the table must say something nice about Dr. Colton," ordered my mother.

There was a long pause and then Anita remarked: "Dr. Colton had a bath last Tuesday."

"I forbid you to say that!" cried my mother.

"Dr. Colton did not have a bath last Tuesday," answered Anita quickly.

My father unfortunately laughed.

My mother, however, did not give up. She was an omnivorous newspaper reader and she planned to have conversation center on some event that had been reported in the press. She also wanted us to get the habit of reading the news, particularly of the political scene, in which she was the most interested.

Sometimes the papers were hard to get hold of, for Minnie read them with equal fervor at night. With two candles lit by her bed, she first turned each page hopefully to see if my father or any member of his family might by some lucky chance be in the news. Then, convinced that there was nothing worth clipping out for her relatives in Sweden, she relaxed into the Harry K. Thaw case and the papers rustled for hours.

Minnie kept most of the Thaw episodes from us, but simpler and bloodier crimes she shared. Sitting on her bed as we picked the tallow from the candles, we discussed with her the strange case of Dr. Crippen. Minnie was absorbed in Dr. Crippen but felt more deeply about his accomplice, Miss Le Neve, whom she thought guiltier.

"What's a paramour, Minnie?"

A paramour was a woman who always ended in the electric chair. Minnie was ready with the chair for any woman mixed up with crime. She resented it when the female sex did not behave well, and she wanted justice to move fast. When Dr. Crippen and Ethel Le Neve arrived on the ship at Quebec disguised as father and son, Minnie was in a fever of excitement. She would have liked to board the boat with the detectives and accuse the dreadful Ethel personally. Dr. Crippen was wicked, but Ethel Le Neve, Minnie was convinced, had single-handedly chopped up Mrs. Crippen.

"Start a topic," said my mother at lunch.

We knew that unless we moved quickly we should be cut out of the conversation entirely and become listeners, a position in which none of us ever wittingly allowed herself to be placed. We also knew that my mother did not admit crime as a topic, though she knew that we knew that she and my father were also reading about the current murder. One or the other of us floundered about with some odd fragment of information, but it did not produce sparkling talk.

Then one morning manna came down from heaven. A perfect news story broke. It began as adventure. It became a mystery. It was one of the great controversies of the time. Blazoned across the papers were the headlines: "Dr. Frederick Cook Discovers the North Pole." Five days later a message was flashed from Indian Harbor, Labrador: "Have made good at last," and Peary declared that he had reached the Pole.

The papers could not arrive early enough. We did not save our views for mealtime. All of us became absorbed in the fantastic story. Was the amiable Dr. Cook a fraud? Three days after his announcement, he arrived in Copenhagen and received a welcome such as the world had never seen. He was in London for a royal audience when he heard the news of Peary.

"There is glory enough for both," said Cook pleasantly.

This already had a fishy smell. Why was he so ready to share his place as the man of the hour? Had the grim Peary been cheated by him of the just reward of the first acclaim? The detractors of Peary asked why he had left Captain Bartlett, his last white assistant, over a hundred miles from the Pole and taken with him for the final dash, as witness, a Negro. One photograph of

Peary and Bartlett shaking hands together at the top of the world would spike any story of a Peary hoax.

The defenders of Peary declared that it was a beautiful, symbolic idea of Peary's that the white man and the black man should make the greatest discovery of the age together. Backwards and forwards went the arguments. Dr. Cook was voluble with the reporters. Peary proudly scorned to argue and stood on his record.

I elected to defend Dr. Cook against all my family. The reasons for this were neither noble nor very complicated. I identified myself with Dr. Cook. He was misunderstood and I was going through a period of feeling very misunderstood myself. I was not so good a swimmer as my sisters and I could not dive. Day after day I jumped from the springboard, holding my nose, amid hoots of ridicule. Alice had had the proud distinction of injuring herself by a double somersault, height sixteen feet. I envied her her wounds. Basely I thought they might be self-inflicted to make her seem important.

Alice came into the dining room and sat down stiffly, the living example of the words that were the most hateful to my ears — "a good sport." I sat opposite her, my hair still wet from my humiliating leaps into the water.

"I tell you, Alice, Dr. Cook gqt there first. Your old Peary never even had the idea till he heard about Cook."

Alice eyed me calmly. "Would you mind passing me the butter. I can't reach it because of my sprained shoulder."

She was the gallant Peary. I was the craven Cook.

11

Deadheads and the Hippodrome

UNTIL I was almost grown-up, I always went to theatrical or musical performances in a second-tier box. It was the custom for professionals to give other professionals boxes, and if Charles Frohman or the Metropolitan Opera Company was giving a production that my father wanted to see, he would merely ask for a box, and the managers in return would be shown the same courtesy for some concert that my father was conducting.

This arrangement made a happy and easy way to go to shows, and it was a great shock to my sisters and me when the time came that we found we had to pay. We had been deadheads for so many years that we had a sense of outrage when we had to give real money — particularly for music. Music had always been free, and the second-tier box was our inalienable right.

If the play was not very good or the pianist not popular, we sat in the first tier, but never in seats. We saw everything from the side, and with the sets of those days we also saw well into the wings. We could see the actor acting and, what was much more interesting, we could see him getting ready to act. When most of the audience thought George, the son, had gone forever and would never, never return, we could observe him in a torn overcoat standing outside waiting for his cue. We saw corpses come alive after they had been dragged off; we watched brokenhearted old ladies suddenly look into mirrors, straighten their hair, and get ready for a curtain call. This gave us a sense of security and also a sense of superiority. Those simple people in ordinary seats were believing it and blowing their noses. We were weeping also, but we were the only ones in the theater who could see it was all pretend.

One of the first plays that I ever saw was *The Squaw Man*, in which William Faversham played the lead. I had never known that life could be so sad or so romantic. I only knew about life from children's books, and suddenly one afternoon I received the wonderful awakening that it would be poignant and lovely to be grown-up. I had never imagined a man like William Faversham. He was so heroic and so handsome, and above everything he suffered so. It seemed to me that I was the only one in the audience who understood his peculiar gallantry.

The Squaw Man tells a story of Honor and Love and Sacrifice. The first scene takes place at Maudsley Towers, where Henry Wynngate, Earl of Kerhill, lives with his wife Diana and his mother, Lady Elizabeth. Henry is obviously a wastrel and is making his wife unhappy. Captain Jim Wynngate — played by Faversham — arrives, and it is soon apparent that he and Diana really love each other but can do nothing about it because of Jim's loyalty to his cousin, the Earl, and above all to the family name. Henry, the Earl, is obviously troubled, and his mother asks him what is ailing him.

After considerable questioning it develops that Henry has, to put it bluntly, absconded with "the Regimental Funds."

Jim gets wind of this crime and makes the heroic gesture of announcing that for the sake of Diana he will leave England so that the guilt will fall on him — thereby preserving in some strange way the honor of the family name. He makes one condition — Henry must give up gambling, "drop Mistress Camille, shut up her establishment," stop all other "miscellaneous liaisons," and be generally nicer to Diana.

Captain Wynngate goes to America, to the Far West; changes his name to Jim Carston and becomes a

tough if rather unsuccessful rancher of cattle, involved
in frequent feuds, and always trying to forget the past.
This is difficult because in the subsequent acts British
officers appear in private cars and guess who Jim Carston is. They insult him and once refuse to allow him
to toast the King. Jim whitens beneath his tan but never
tells. A young Indian girl called Nat-U-Rich, with long
black braids, who speaks only in monosyllables, shoots
a man to save Jim's life.

The years roll by, seven of them; Jim's hair silvers a
bit at the temples, but otherwise he remains his handsome, gallant self. Then one evening, who should come
to the broken-down ranch house from England but
Petrie, the old family solicitor. He recognizes Jim after
some piercing looks from under his shaggy white eye-
brows. He then calls him "Milord" and says he has
made this long journey to inform him that Henry, the
Earl of Kerhill, is dead.

Petrie urges Jim to return to England and assume his
rightful place as Earl of Kerhill, head of the house. He
hints that Diana is waiting.

From here on the play becomes very lush. The sky
turns pink and the orchestra strikes up in tremulo a
melody of Sordini. Jim gazes at the desolate ranch house
and makes a broken speech on how homesick he is for
England, for Maudsley Towers "with its thousand-year-

old oaks," for the respectful servants, for all the little customs that only an exiled Britisher understands and yearns for.

At this moment a child's voice cries from off stage, "Daddy — Daddy," and a boy of about five with very blond hair and dressed in an Indian suit runs onto the stage and into Jim's arms. At the same time Nat-U-Rich, the Indian squaw, comes out of the door of the ranch house, gazes searchingly at Petrie, and then walks out toward the mountain with her hands crossed over her chest. We all shivered with surprise and shock at this development.

Jim tells Petrie, the solicitor, that this is his son Hal; that he married Nat-U-Rich so that Hal would not "be branded with illegitimacy," and this is the result of his loneliness. He can never leave. He is tied to the squaw.

Petrie, after his first horror at this turn of events, reminds Jim that Hal, though part Indian, is still the heir to the Earldom. Hal should return to England with Petrie and be educated as befits his rank.

After a brief and tortured struggle, Jim agrees and tries to explain to Nat-U-Rich in pidgin English that Hal is to be taken away from her. At this moment, Diana walks into the scene, having come to America as a surprise, and the unfortunate Nat-U-Rich, obviously upset by all these developments, pulls a revolver from out of her bosom and shoots herself. Jim picks her up in his arms, dead, while Diana murmurs "poor little mother" and puts her arms protectingly around little Hal.

As can be seen, it was a very unhappy happy ending. Diana, like Mrs. Pinkerton in *Madame Butterfly*, was not a sympathetic character, and something Fourth of July rebelled in me that an American squaw wasn't considered good enough to be an English countess. But I never blamed William Faversham. Through it all he seemed to me a complete hero.

I spent many hours thinking of his life with Diana and little Hal. I so believed the play that I imagined he was really back at Maudsley Towers with the respectful servants, walking under those thousand-year-old oaks. I had one picture of him that I had cut out of a newspaper, very blurred, with Nat-U-Rich kneeling at his feet. I clipped Nat-U-Rich out of the picture so that I might contemplate Faversham undisturbed by the squaw. This gave his extended arms a rather meaningless look — but not for long, for in the hole I inserted a snapshot of myself. The proportions were askew, Faversham looking as though he had a midget in a sailor suit between his arms, but to me it looked — right.

One morning at breakfast I received in the mail a

glossy picture postcard of Faversham, shirt open at the throat, and across it written in black ink, "To Gretchen, Ever Truly Yours, William Faversham." I was thunderstruck. How did he know my feelings? How did he even know of my existence? Perhaps he had seen me in the second-tier box and made inquiries. He was a friend of my father's. That must be the explanation. I asked my father in what I felt was a casual manner if he had ever happened to discuss me with Mr. Faversham. My father said he couldn't imagine in what connection, but I knew better. I analyzed and reanalyzed the meaning of the words "Ever Truly Yours." It was more intimate than "Sincerely." It went pretty far when one realized that it was on a postcard that anyone could read.

And yet though I kept that card on my bureau and looked at it morning and night, it was not enough to live on. When Alice told me several months later she had sent it, I no longer cared. Faversham had come to dinner and brought his handsome wife. He had talked to me about his children, who must be "about your age." He had been faithless to Nat-U-Rich, Diana, Hal — and me.

The plays that we saw drove their points home very, very clearly. The characters paid for their actions, and the wages of sin were unmistakable and unvarnished. There were many bad men in the theater who remained untamed until the last act.

In *The Great Divide* I suspected early that Ghent possessed a noble heart, though he had purchased the girl Ruth against her will by throwing a bag of gold nuggets down on the table, and was about to drag her off with him, as his, by sale.

RUTH. But — *how* yours? Oh remember, have pity! *How* yours?
GHENT. Bought if you like, but mine! Mine by blind chance and the hell in a man's veins, if you like!

With sudden intuition I whispered to my sisters that he *really* loved her and I *thought* she was going to love him.

The Dawn of a Tomorrow was the height of sophistication. One act was played in Oliver Holt's Chambers. Oliver was the gay and demoralized nephew of rich old Sir Oliver Holt and he was waiting hopefully for his uncle to die. He gave a party in his Chambers — exciting word, no American possessed that kind of home — and the first arrival was Lord Tommy.

Lord Tommy asked who else was coming. Oliver said Madge Delorne was expected. They analyzed Madge as they got out the champagne.

"In any case — she's a deuced clever woman — Madge Delorne."

When Madge arrived in a low-cut evening dress, the corks popped and Lord Tommy sat at the piano and sang "The Owl and the Pussy Cat."

> They took some honey, and plenty of money
> Wrapped up in a five-pound note.

This innuendo about the expected inheritance was ignored by Oliver, who was kissing Madge's shoulder. Madge told him not to be a brute.

"You're rather a brute yourself, you know, Madge — in your own alluring way."

Then a little later the door of the Chambers burst open and Glad, the slum girl, with flaming red hair and dressed in rags, came in. Glad was the waif who had been kicked around but had never lost her hope. "I'm alive and there's always tomorrow!"

Glad was played by Eleanor Robson, and she brought reality and heart to the role. When she was on the stage she galvanized the scenes. The audience believed her loyalty to her slum companion, the Dandy, her naïve goodness to Sir Oliver. She turned a sentimental evening into something dramatic.

Occasionally the theater was used for improvement. My mother and father had apparently concluded that anything that was in verse, that was in costume, that was tragic, and that was *long*, must be educational. Also there were plenty of boxes available for this kind of show. My parents were too canny to let themselves in for an endless afternoon of rhyme, so we would be sent with Minnie, my father assuring us that he had seen the play a few years before, or as a boy, and that it was charming. What was the story? He wouldn't spoil it for us by telling the story. It would take away the surprise.

We saw in this way *Brand*, by Ibsen, and *The Sunken Bell*, by Hauptmann. Both were in five acts, and the plots were completely incomprehensible to us. Brand's efforts to throw off the heritage of wrong and atone for his mother's sin, illustrated by lengthy soliloquies overheard only by God, we could make neither head nor tail of. It wasn't our idea of a surprise.

The Sunken Bell was a little better because more happened. There was a character called "The Nickel-mann," a water spirit who lived in a well. He always announced that he was coming up from the well by crying "Brekekekex!" We laughed at this loudly. There was a maiden called Rautendelein, who sat on the edge of the well combing her golden hair as she made a long speech to a bee: —

Thou buzzing, golden wight — whence com'st thou
    here? . . .

What? — loit'ring still? Away — away with thee!
Am I a rose bush? . . . Are my lips a rose? . . .
Hey! Chimney! Puff some smoke across the glade,
To drive away this naughty wilful bee.

My sisters and I looked at each other in an embarrassed way and Minnie groaned.

Heinrich, the bell-founder, had been stolen from his wife, Magda, by Rautendelein assisted by Trolds and dwarfs. The story picked up considerably when Magda tried to get Heinrich back, the Trolds being nice and bad. Minnie groaned several times in a different way over the Trolds.

We acted *The Sunken Bell* at home, constructing a well behind the sofa. Polly climbed out with water on her face, saying, "Brekekekekex — Brekekekekex." Then we went on with the play in what we felt was improved and zippier Hauptmann dialogue.

There was one event to which we always went in seats — bought seats. This was the New York Hippodrome. The Hippodrome was the big treat of the winter. It was to us the finest form of entertainment. It was something to anticipate for months, to reflect on for the rest of the year.

In the first place it was such a satisfactory length. The matinee began about one-thirty — at least we were always in our seats by then — and at six o'clock it ended. You went into the Hippodrome in sunlight, and when you came out there were stars in the sky. But you had lived in those hours through a lifetime of adventure. You had been to foreign lands, at a circus, under the sea, in a balloon. You had watched battles, seen ballets, and laughed yourself into stitches over the clown Marceline.

When one entered the Hippodrome, two senses were immediately challenged. The lobby was decorated with great elephants' heads with gold tusks, and on the end of each tusk was an electric bulb — lighted. And coming up the stairs from the basement was a smell of real elephant. Here we always paused — to look at those gold and illuminated tusks, to reassure ourselves by the smell that all was right.

The performance was divided into three parts. It began with "A Spectacular Drama" in a number of scenes played in many parts of the globe. The cast was enormous, but the story was comparatively easy to follow. I particularly remember the year in which the drama *Around the World* was given.

The first scene opened at an estate on the Hudson where rich Mr. Burlingham in a frock coat and silk hat was giving a party for his beautiful daughter Cynthia. Among the guests were an English Lord, a French Count, and an American Naval Lieutenant. As the

Lord had a monocle, the audience knew immediately that he was a comic character, particularly because when the monocle fell into his coffee cup he reinserted it into his eye wet and brown and then accused his host of being a Blackamoor. The Count, being French, was naturally a villain, and it was a pretty good guess that the Naval Lieutenant would become the hero. Mr. Burlingham invited the group, which included some other gentlemen and ladies, to join his daughter and himself on a yachting trip around the world.

In the subsequent scenes the Burlingham party had many adventures, but the wonder of the trip lay in the fact that every place the group visited looked exactly as one had been led to suppose it ought to look.

Scene II.   *The Yacht in Mid-Ocean.*
Scene III.   *Garden Party at Windsor Castle.*

The English Lord entertained the Burlinghams on the lawn, having borrowed the Castle and grounds for the afternoon.

Scene IV.   *Switzerland. The Alps.*
Scene V.   *Egypt. The Sphinx. Daybreak in the Desert.*

The French Count tried to kidnap Cynthia and the Naval Lieutenant knocked him down and rescued her.

Scene VI.   *The Sandstorm.*

Real sand was blown over everybody.

Scene VII.   *Constantinople. Garden of the Vizier's Harem.*
Scene VIII.   *India. The Durbar.*

The English Lord borrowed the Durbar and entertained the Burlinghams on real elephants.

Scene IX.   *Italy. Venice — by Moonlight.*

Here the French Count sat with a group of Italians in a gondola and serenaded Cynthia. Dark and apparently genuine clouds moved swiftly over the sky. Suddenly the clouds parted, showing an enormous crescent moon, on the end of which sat the Naval Lieutenant. A real American song burst from his lips, the first four lines being: —

> Moon, dear
>   don't shine too soon, dear,
> And when we spoon, dear,
>   Then hide your light.[1]

At the conclusion he threw Cynthia a rose which she caught.

[1] Copyright 1925, M. Witmark & Sons. Used by permission.

Scene X.   Spain. The Bull Ring in Seville.

The final scene was played in *Ireland at Blarney Castle*, with a Kissing Stone and a Wishing Well.

A jig was danced by a large group and in the middle of it, dressed in a green coat and stovepipe hat, whirled the American Lieutenant, who sang that he was really an Irishman and would Cynthia be his little colleen. The audience broke into happy applause and — the curtain fell.

The second part of the performance was given over to a circus and entirely dominated by Marceline. He was a Spanish clown who played deaf and dumb, and who was always in trouble because of an overwhelming desire to help the circus along.

When the men appeared to set up the ring, Marceline pulled each peg out as it was hammered down and ran ahead with it to the man in front. To the ecstasy of the audience the men never caught on and they would have to set up the ring three times. When the carpet was unrolled for the ponies, Marceline rolled it up again just before the ponies appeared. Marceline pulled a net out from under the highest trapeze artist as he was preparing to drop down, and folded it neatly away, thinking the act was over.

The manager appeared in a red coat and high hat and

protested in a loud voice. He gesticulated, he pointed up at the trapeze. Did Marceline understand! This was the Dip of Death! He must leave the net alone! Marceline looked at the manager's gestures, pointed at the figure above, pointed at himself, shook his head, then nodded and smiled. Yes, he understood.

The drums rolled again. The Dip Artist started swinging and then at the very moment he was about to plunge, Marceline jumped forward, pulled at a rope, and net and all fell on the manager in a wild tangle, knocking him over, while the trapezist by a lucky chance caught another swing. The audience rocked with laughter. Trust Marceline!

It was the third part of the Hippodrome that was the climax. Here was displayed the great feature, the Tank — truly described as the hydraulic marvel of the age. The stage was filled with actual water and the marvel lay in the fact that when human beings dived or walked down into the water, *they never came up again*. I do not expect to be believed for this statement, but I can only swear that my sisters and I would stand up in our seats to find out what had happened. We saw mermaids being chased by sailors, we saw them disappear into the water — a few bubbles, *and that was all*. No one floated up to the surface. The mermaids wore a good deal and the sailors possibly had weights in their pockets which may have accounted for their bodies' remaining at the bottom of the Tank. But it gave a ghoulish zest to the end of the show to think how many lives were being sacrificed.

The Tank was filled in the second intermission and we always cut short our visit to the animals in the basement when we heard the first sounds of gushing water. By the time the Tank was two-thirds full the whole audience was there waiting excitedly for the strange disappearances. Usually the water was used as a finale for a spectacle. Neptune floated in on a heavily decorated raft and blew a horn. Then down some great steps appeared his court, and in fours marched right into the water and out of sight. Before the final view I noticed that the water spirits wore a set expression around the jaw and took a deep breath. The climax came when Neptune, beard dripping, followed them down and was gone forever.

One of the earliest performances of the Hippodrome took place a few months after the conclusion of the Russo-Japanese War. Throughout the country sympathy was weighted in favor of the Japanese. The demands of Tsar Nicholas II seemed excessive; he had grabbed Port Arthur and was about to seize Korea. The Japanese attempted a settlement, but the Russian government, anxious to distract their masses from revolutionary activity at home, refused to negotiate and remained uncompromising. Americans did not like the Tsar and "his Cossacks," and made up a phrase which swept the country: "The Japanese are wonderful little people."

When Port Arthur fell to the Japanese, there was great enthusiasm. The Hippodrome saw its opportunity. It put on a big spectacle called *Battle of Port Arthur* and used in it three regiments of soldiers, a naval ship, artillery fire, and for the grand climax a wild dash of live horses into the tank. The story of the spectacle was so important — and complicated — that the management presented in the program an outline of what the audience must watch for.

BATTLE OF PORT ARTHUR

The first scene shows the beleaguered city. Beyond the great wall are the snow-capped hills that are soon to be reddened with blood. A prison pen is crowded with Japanese women. The street is thronged with women begging for bread. They become riotous and a Cossack charge drives them away. The commanding general arrives with bread. Troops come in and drill and give exhibitions of wall scaling. The Cossacks and other cavalry indulge in the skillful sports of soldier horsemen. Japanese spies circulate among soldiers and peasantry.

A captured Japanese officer is brought in and imprisoned. A courier gallops on with a message calling for reinforcements. The troops are assembled and the spectator watches with wonder the march to the front, infantry, artillery, and cavalry. The gates of the city are closed and the spies release the prisoners. A bomb bursts in a small house, shattering it and leaving it ablaze. The attack grows heavier, roll after roll of musketry is heard above the rattle of machine guns. Presently there is a wild shout. The Russians are in retreat. Troops rush in still firing at the pursuers. An artillery piece is placed near the gate and belches forth a deafening fire. The hospital corps come on with the wounded. With a fearful yell the entire cavalry retreats through the gate while the attacking party presses on.

A THRILLING BATTLE FOUGHT IN THE RAIN

The second scene shows 203 Mitre Hill. The Russians are in possession. There is a fort at the top while beneath there is a rocky plateau, the edges of which are washed by the waters of a lake. Here the enormous tank, at which engineers the world over have marveled, is shown to its best advantage. It is night. Sentries make their silent patrol while the troops, knowing naught of what day or dawn may bring, slumber uneasily among the rocks. An auxiliary gunboat floats about the lake, sweeping the hill with its searchlight. A Japanese party under a flag of truce discuss terms with Russia's commandant. They are refused.

"Let your Colonel come himself," says the Russian general.

"He will come," replies the aide, "and at his back will come the army of Japan!"

There is a call to arms. The hill is then crowded with soldiers. Wildly shouting, Cossack cavalry rush across the rocky way for the assembly. A shot is heard and instantly the flagpole falls with a crash. A Japanese spy tries to stab the commanding officer but he is shot, and falling into the lake, *rises no more*.

The attack at long range becomes a hand to hand conflict. Japanese rush on, fighting over the rocks. Machine guns keep up a heavy return fire on the fort. A shell strikes the gunboat and it sinks with all on board.

Japanese infantry drive the Russians from the rocky fastnesses and, screaming their "Banzais," scale the wall of the fort and place the Mikado's flag upon its ramparts. It is raining like fury and the spectators are witnessing a battle fought in the rain. The Russians retreat and for a sensational climax the Cossack cavalry, in a mad gallop, cross the rocks and plunge into the lake. Cheers and deafening applause echo through the vast auditorium for the greatest battle spectacle of the age has thrilled as no theatric and mimic representation of the grandeur of war has ever done before.

As my dazed sisters and I stumbled up the aisle, having remained for every curtain call, we were all thinking the same thoughts. Which one of us had enough allowance saved to do a repeat on *Battle of Port Arthur*? Which aunt or uncle could be inspired to make the generous gesture? And how could we persuade my mother of the obvious fact that to be able to go to the same performance next week would be twice as wonderful as seeing it for the first time; we could anticipate the bliss ahead — the Cossacks drowning in the Tank.

12

Ship's Auction

TRAVELING with my father was always comfortable and efficient, particularly if there were not too many sisters along. If one was alone with my father one shared equally in all the services that sprang up at his appearance. Drawing rooms on trains were found for him when all had supposedly been reserved by other people; and when the orchestra was with him, engineers made special stops and whole timetables were altered.

My father and I had one trait in common; we liked to arrive in plenty of time to catch a train. Neither of us was capable of being late. The morning that we knew we were going on a journey we were in a nervous fever of excitement for several hours before we had to go to the station.

One year I went with my father to Saratoga Springs, where he was to conduct a pair of concerts. The orchestra had gone the day before on a special train and we were to follow the next day on the 10.00 A.M. We breakfasted at a quarter to eight and at ten of nine were at the station in time to catch the earlier train for Saratoga, the 9.05. This pleased my father: it was proof positive that we were on time. I was for taking the first train, but my father liked to stick to what he called "the arrangements." He bought the papers which we had read at breakfast and said that we could amuse ourselves by "studying human nature." We studied human nature for four minutes and were done with it. The 9.05 had not yet gone and we still had a chance to make it, but my father did not trust it. It wasn't his train. So we waited the hour, caught the ten o'clock, and were standing in the aisle, ready to get out again, a good twenty minutes before the train reached Saratoga.

My mother took a chance on any journey. It never bothered her if she had no reservations. She climbed into an upper berth or sat up all night and took it all very casually. If there was a stopover of a couple of hours, she went sight-seeing. She drove out in a cab to see the waterfalls or the outside of the new insane asylum while my father waited agitatedly at the station looking anxiously every few minutes at his big gold watch. My father had more confidence in his watch than in station clocks, which he claimed ran about ten minutes slow.

My father traveled so much and so far on his tours with the orchestra that he associated train trips with work. To my mother a trip was adventure and an escape from home and children. As a result, their attitudes were very different. My father, knowing he had a schedule with a number of one-night stands, followed the timetable carefully. But he tried to make himself as comfortable as possible. He often sent a bottle of wine into the dining car to be iced for dinner, and he liked to discuss with the steward what might be specially cooked for him. Trout appeared at his table alone, and the salad was mixed according to his directions.

All this was too much like home for my mother. She ordered a chop and a baked potato for her first meal and never varied the order through thirty-five states. In vain did my father try to argue her into eating something different. My mother wanted to get back to the book she finally had time to read, or jump out at the next station for a seven-minute look down the town's main street. My mother and father both liked traveling, but for quite different reasons.

It was on an ocean voyage that my father really relaxed. The arrangements had been made; there was no timetable to study, and he could give himself over to amusing himself with human nature and enjoying his popularity with the passengers and crew. Particularly did my father blossom on the French Line.

The Compagnie Générale Transatlantique was to us, as to many other Americans, the most remarkable line that existed, and we helped support it for many years. We had been on British boats but we never had so good a time. The English were apparently determined to make us remember we were on the ocean. Their boat drills were serious and genuine affairs. A lady, except for first place in the lifeboat, seemed to have no privileges. She was kept out of smoking rooms and bars and was allowed in only one *salon*, where she could drink tea. No English passengers spoke to us or even to fellow Britishers without an introduction. I used to wonder whether, if we and the English landed in a lifeboat together, after the third day of washing around we would break the ice and shake hands. I never was sure.

An English ship seemed designed to keep people apart. The passengers liked privacy and that was the last thing my sisters and I wanted on a voyage. The English made us feel younger than we were, and on a boat for a week each of us wanted to add at least three years.

With the French Line, from the moment we stepped on board it was gala, gala. The French tried to conceal from their passengers the fact that they were at sea. Sometimes there were life preservers in the cabin, often not. A sign pointed to *Canot de Sauvetage,* but if one followed the sign, the lifeboat might not be there at all. If there was a whistle for a boat drill, passengers might lift their faces from their *Vermouth Cassis* to wonder what the noise was about, but it was a sign of a complete lack of sophistication to go anywhere.

I humiliated myself on an early trip by appearing tied into a life preserver, on Pont B. Standing there were a bored stewardess, a nurse, and a child. That was all. Covered with shame, I rushed back to my cabin. I had done the unpardonable; I had not been sophisticated. How my sisters would laugh at me if they knew.

One reason for the success of the French Line was the illusion that it gave to all its passengers that they had a special drag. Businessmen, students, buyers, felt that the Compagnie Générale Transatlantique knew that they were *les grands amis de la France* and wanted to recognize this fact by bettering their cabins. A long line formed outside the purser's office, and for three days everyone changed accommodations. Somehow the pursers, from Monsieur Latour-Maigret down, gave the passengers the illusion that their claims were recognized and something immediately would be done about them. If the cabin one had originally been given had Art Moderne *décor*, one was moved to an identical cabin, *décor* Louis Seize. All decks played a kind of gigantic "Going to Jerusalem," and seized each other's places.

There was one group that did have a special pull and whose claims were genuinely recognized. These were the artists. The French loved and understood the musicians and the actors, and no cabin was considered too good for them. Pianists, conductors, or leading ladies, from the moment they stepped on board, were treated with particular attention and flattery. What was more, judgments of the worth of an artist were very genuine. Señor Arbós, for example, the Spanish conductor, on his first trip to America, received a bigger cabin than the newest star of the movies, though the star earned ten times as much as Señor Arbós.

The ship's concerts had a list of performers that rivaled Paris or New York. The piano was always in tune, and somehow the man who thought he could whistle and the lady who was determined to sing "Home, Home, from the Hills" were eliminated and a delighted, though often an intoxicated, audience heard and cheered Paul Kochanski or Artur Rubinstein.

One August my father found that he had to return from Europe earlier than he had planned, and brought Polly back with him. Later each one gave a version of the trip, and though the two stories differed it was possible to piece together what had happened.

The ship was the *France*, the handsomest of the

French Line. Monsieur Latour-Maigret was the purser, and when my father appeared at his office, Monsieur Latour-Maigret embraced him with joy and then threw up his hands in despair over his problems of cabin assignments. The boat was too crowded on this trip. *Le bureau à Paris* had made a dozen mistakes, having sold the same space several times over.

Monsieur Latour-Maigret of course immediately found a better cabin for my father, with private bath — but for Mademoiselle Pollee, *très, très difficile*. Would she consent to share a cabin with Mademoiselle Piccard, *une chanteuse ravissante*, and in two days, *parole d'honneur*, a perfect single cabin would present itself.

Polly looked at the arrangement with some misgivings, for her French was weak, particularly in verbs and high numbers, though she made a constant effort to be idiomatic. She had seen in her French reading the expression *hein*, which she used frequently but pronounced it to rhyme with "fine." If she could survive the language difficulties with Mademoiselle Piccard, the cabin presented a definite advantage. It was on a lower deck than my father's and so would give her greater independence.

Polly was adding the customary three years for the trip. She had several new dresses from Paris and some belonging to her sisters that she was taking home for them. She planned to wear them all in rotation so that she could assure the customs in New York that they were old stuff. It was a point of honor for all of us to get as much as possible through the customs without declaration. In Polly's shoes were little bottles of liqueurs, and perfume was hidden in hats and in the pockets and linings of her coat. When she walked, she clinked like John Gilpin.

When Polly arrived at the cabin, Mademoiselle Piccard was already lying in the lower berth with a thick cream spread over her face. Polly was not sure if she was awake, so she climbed into the upper berth as quietly as possible. A guttural voice spoke.

"Croyez-vous en Dieu, Mademoiselle?"

"Croyez-vous?" asked Polly anxiously.

"Naturellement, mais en même temps — "

"Bon soir," said Polly determinedly.

The next day Mademoiselle Piccard had herself moved to another cabin, having found conversation with Polly unrewarding.

Captain Jacquemot immediately asked my father and Polly to sit at his table. Captain Jacquemot was a handsome Breton with black hair and dark eyes and possessed a fine tenor voice. He loved to sing, and late at night when the bar and *salon* were nearly deserted he would leave the bridge and perform happily with the musicians who were on the trip. He also liked to dance and play bridge, and his dark eye was well aware of which women who were making the voyage were *jolies, délicieuses,* or *formidables.*

Captain Jacquemot was enchanted with Polly. Polly possessed an eerie quality which only exasperated my father — he never could make out if she understood the point he was making or was merely giving him her wide smile and thinking of something else. But Captain Jacquemot became convinced that Mademoiselle Pollee grasped every one of his best nuances. He placed her opposite to him, then on his left, then on his right, and he constantly lifted his glass to her. He believed or did not believe her alleged age — but he was interested in the variety of costumes that Polly was conscientiously wearing, some so wintry, some so springlike, and he improved her French in a soft undertone.

The chief steward would bend his head close to Captain Jacquemot while they discussed whether the *Bombe Glacée* or the *Crêpes Suzette Flambées* would interest Mademoiselle Pollee more. Then the *sommelier,* his neck covered with chains, would bend over to the other side and murmur, *"Parfaitement, mon Capitaine,"* as Captain Jacquemot ordered *un vin rosé un peu mousseux* which he believed Polly would like. The *sommelier* would disappear and bring the special bottle, and after pouring a little into Captain Jacquemot's glass would pour a great deal into Polly's glass. Then Captain Jacquemot would raise his glass and the toasts began.

Each night a different guest at the Captain's table ordered a special wine as a present to the other guests. Besides my father and Polly, there were an actress from the Comédie, a French Industrialist, Mordkin of the Russian Ballet, and some Americans who said they were Steel, and Copper, and Sugar Refining, Inc., and they all became very gay and lively. Polly of course found this delightful. Muffled in fur or swathed in chiffon, depending on which sister's dress she was aging, she lifted her glass to Steel and Copper while the steward pressed on her ice hollowed in the shape of a swan in which there was caviar, and invariably she and Captain Jacquemot clinked their *rosé* together and ended the dinner with *Crêpes Suzette*.

One evening the Captain asked Polly if there was anything further that he could do for her pleasure.

"*Oui*," said Polly suddenly, "*je voudrais bien voir un iceberg*."

Captain Jacquemot was startled. The ship was nowhere near the icebergs. He raised his glass again to Polly: "*Pour vous je ferais n'importe quoi!*"

Polly lay in her berth and studied the ship's newspaper. First she read the leading article, *Les Parfums de*

Grasse. Then she turned to the second page, *Le Maroc, Pays Féerique du Soleil*. This was illustrated by a blurred photograph of a bearded old man in a fez. Opposite this was another long piece, *Baudelaire — Poète de la Venus Noire*. On the next page there was a heading *Dernière Heure* and under it a brief account of what was happening in England and China. Under this in larger type came the heading *La Bourse* with four stock quotations. Next came a heading, *Le Sport. Le Shuffle et Le Deck Tennis à 3 heures*. Finally, in very large type, appeared the words: *Gala, Gala, Gala. Diner du Capitaine; Ship's Auction — M. Walter Damrosch.*

My father was considered the top auctioneer on any voyage and he was invariably invited for this exhausting role. He had the record for raising more money *pour la Société Maritime des Veuves et Orphelins* than any other passenger, and the francs poured in when he went to work. He was justifiably proud of his talent in this direction and he described his methods to Polly as they paced the deck before the Captain's dinner. Polly had never seen my father in the role of auctioneer — in fact had never attended an auction — and she was of course excited at the prospect.

"The important thing," my father told her, "is to keep the bidding open. Never let anything be knocked down too quickly. Persuade someone to push it another hundred francs and you're off again and can run it way up."

Polly listened with deep interest to the words of the master.

"Oh, I hope it will go well tonight," she said.

"Don't worry," laughed my father confidently. "All I have to find is some co-operative jackass who won't let go and will keep on bidding. That's all I need."

"You'll find one," declared Polly.

The Captain's table was strewn with flowers, and the menu, looking like an invitation to a royal wedding, took up two pages. It began with *Caviar de Sterlet* and *Crêpes de Sarrasin*, went through *Baron d'Agneau de Lait, Asperge de Serre, Sauce Mousseline*, and ended with *Pêche de Montreuil, Belle Dijonnaise*. My father, who had been in consultation with the wine steward in a series of thoughtful meetings, was giving the champagne — Lanson 1904. The first magnum arrived with the dessert and the toasts began.

"À *la grande amitié entre la France et l'Amérique!*" Everyone stood up. "À *la santé de Mademoiselle Dorziat, artiste superbe!*" The champagne was making a hit and my father looked about the table happily. Then his eye fell on Polly. She was smiling over her glass at Sugar Refining, Inc., and in her glass was the *vin rosé*. He signaled to her quickly to drink champagne. Polly merely raised her *vin rosé* to him.

After dinner my father walked the deck again with Polly. He was perturbed.

"Do you realize what I was giving the table to drink tonight?" he asked.

"Champagne," said Polly.

"Not just champagne — Lanson 1904. One of the finest marks in the world. You refused it!"

"I like the *rosé*," declared Polly.

"I want you to promise me something," said my father earnestly. "I want you to promise me that never again, as long as you live, will you refuse Lanson 1904."

And Polly quite truthfully promised that she never would.

My father faced the large crowd of first-class passengers. Behind him on a long table were the donations to be auctioned: perfume, wine, autographed pictures of celebrities, three handbags, a doll, an embroidered sweater, some wooden bears from Switzerland, some white pigeons fastened to an alabaster bowl from Florence, a Spanish shawl — all the vast variety of tourist purchases, including a little Reboux hat.

Polly sat at a table in the corner with Mademoiselle Piccard, the French Industrialist, and Steel, sipping a green mint as she watched the scene with great curiosity. My father after some flattering remarks to the audience picked up his first item, a pair of lady's gloves. He ran them up to three hundred francs and then suggested that Mademoiselle Piccard stand up and wear one glove to show the audience its remarkable shape. The audience applauded Mademoiselle Piccard loudly as she held up her gloved hand. My father then refused to take any bids from the ladies. Only the men were to be allowed to vie with each other in securing *ces gants élégants*. They were finally knocked down for a thousand francs.

From then on the bidding grew lively. Perfumes brought the prices of liqueurs. A picture was held up with a scarf placed over it and my father challenged the audience to secure an unseen masterpiece. He then turned the picture around, pulled up the scarf, and examined it himself. Then he gasped and faced his public.

"All I can tell you, ladies and gentlemen, is that it combines the best of Raphael and El Greco, with a *soupçon* of *La Vie Parisienne*. I will not reveal to you the subject of the picture. Is it old Greece? Is it the female form divine? Is it rugged nature? Only the lucky winner will find this out!"

"Is the artist living or dead?" a man cried out.

My father lifted a corner of the scarf again and peered

at the signature with a puzzled expression. The crowd gave a big laugh.

"I cannot tell you that," said my father, "but the picture is immortal!"

The francs and dollars were raised against each other. The picture was finally knocked down to an excited lady.

"You must look at it alone in your cabin," commanded my father, "and then charge fifty francs admission to those who wish to see it. La Société Maritime des Veuves et Orphelins will naturally receive the usual 10 per cent commission."

Captain Jacquemot and Monsieur Latour-Maigret looked happily at each other. The *France* was beating every liner on the lake tonight.

My father held up the Reboux hat. The audience, exhausted with its efforts to secure the painting, began the bidding languidly.

"Twenty-five francs."

"Twenty-five francs for this handbag — I mean hat," expostulated my father. "Look at it, ladies and gentlemen."

It was a small toque with an overblown rose tucked into the tulle. There was a long pause; the hat did not appeal.

"Come, come," exclaimed my father, "the petals will fall if someone doesn't buy it quickly and put it into water."

"*Cinquante francs,*" said a man.

Polly saw her opportunity. Now was a chance to help my father. She took a sip of the mint and cleared her throat.

"*Cinq cents francs,*" she cried.

The audience buzzed and craned their necks. My father had not recognized the voice.

"There, you see. Someone realizes the value of this remarkable little concoction. Five hundred francs — are you going to let it go so cheaply?"

"*Sept cents francs,*" bid the Industrialist at Polly's table.

"*Un mille!*" exclaimed Polly, delighted at the interest her bidding was creating. My father had suddenly turned and was looking at her. She waved cheerfully back at him. She wanted him to know that she was right there filling the vacuum he had dreaded — she was the man who was going to keep the bidding open.

Steel now entered the arena.

"Fifteen hundred francs," he cried. But Polly wanted to do her raising in French.

"*Deux mille,*" she shouted back.

"*C'est formidable!*" exclaimed a group.

My father was flabbergasted. He was justifiably convinced Polly did not understand the principle of an auction. He was equally certain she could not count correctly in such high figures in French. He knew that ultimately he would have to pay the bill. He wanted to get the hat into the hands of someone else and knock it down quickly.

"*Deux mille,*" he repeated. He turned hopefully to Steel. "I am sure the gentleman here — if he wanted this ravishing little hat before — will want it even more ardently, now that there is competition. Do I hear twenty-five hundred? Do I hear twenty-three hundred — ?"

The Industrialist jumped in again.

"*Deux mille, deux cent cinquante,*" he announced.

"Going — going — " cried my father, rapping with his gavel.

"Twenty-five hundred," yelled Steel.

"*Trois mille,*" screamed Polly.

There was applause and laughter. The audience liked the competition. Polly gazed proudly at my father. She had never seen him so excited. His face was enflamed. His voice actually shook with his next remark.

"We can't let this priceless hat go for a mere three thousand. If one of these gentlemen really wants it, I will knock it down to him quickly. Do I hear something?"

"Thirty-two hundred," said Steel.

"*Trois mille, cinq cents!*" cried Polly.

"Do I hear another bid?" begged my father looking agonizedly at the Industrialist. "Is Monsieur satisfied to leave it at thirty-five hundred?"

There was a silence.

"Only thirty-five hundred," protested my father, looking with ill-disguised hatred at the rose-draped toque.

"*Quatre mille!*" called Polly triumphantly.

This was too much for my father. Polly was now bidding against herself. He thought rapidly. What would she do next? Dare he leave it open once more on the faint hope that someone else would speak and he would close the deal before she had time to move, or would she jump herself again?

"This adorable little hat is about to be sold. Is there a last bid?" Knock went the gavel and my father paused for a hopeful second. Then he saw Polly's hand go up and her mouth open.

"Going — gone!" and my father brought the gavel down with increasing rapidity. "Sold for four thousand francs!"

There was long and loud applause. Polly blushed with pride and pleasure as the hat was brought to her. A steward appeared and asked her for the small formality of signing a little paper. Polly wrote my father's name and the number of his cabin. Then she went into the grand *salon* to dance the tango with the Industrialist.

The next morning my father and Polly again paced the deck. My father began a comprehensive talk on money — money that was yours, and money that wasn't yours; on debts and the rapidity with which they caught up with one; and a gala at night on a ship was a particularly dangerous time to risk somebody else's — that is, your father's — money.

"But I only did it to help you," protested Polly.

"Promise me something," said my father. "Promise me you will never, never help me again!" And he gazed out to sea with a martyred look.

The weather had turned surprisingly chilly. Two passengers passed with their coat collars turned up and one remarked that he couldn't understand it, it looked as though the ship were way off its course.

"Can you wear the damned hat?" asked my father.

"It's too tight," said Polly.

This threw my father into an even deeper depression. They continued along the deck and walked slowly under the bridge. Suddenly Captain Jacquemot sprang out and waved at them.

"*Mademoiselle Pollee*," he shouted, "*je suis un homme d'honneur. Regardez!*"

There on the port side of the *France* floated a great green iceberg. Captain Jacquemot was joined by two other officers who watched with pleasure Polly's happiness — happiness at the change of subject.

"*C'est magnifique — hine?*" cried Polly, looking up at them.

The *France* docked five hours late in New York.

13

The Consorts

IN FICTION and in many biographies, musicians are pictured as tempestuous characters, great lovers, careless of their appearance, late to their engagements, lost in a dream world of creation, with no head for finance, out of contact with everyday life, speaking all languages with a heavy accent, and living in studios with moss-green walls, or garrets, or the *palazzo* of some Contessa.

That is as may be. I cannot speak for other times. I also know the story of Chopin and George Sand; of Liszt and the Countess D'Agoult. They belonged in the nineteenth century, the romantic century. But I have suspected that biographers have colored their stories, that there are holes which if filled in would make Chopin or Liszt not so unlike an artist of today.

There is a picture which has been printed in many magazines in black and white and in color, to advertise a perfume. I have a sneaking fondness for this picture — it is so very romantic — but I do not believe it. It shows a young woman at the piano and a violinist beside her. A climax has come in the music which has so moved the violinist that he stops his playing and passionately kisses the pianist as her hands still rest on the keys. This is, I believe, an impossible situation.

It is fair to assume that they are playing a sonata, let us say the Brahms D Minor, because only great music could inspire such feelings. In a sonata the pianist and the violinist are equals — one does not accompany the other. Therefore they have the same rights. Now to play a sonata well, the two musicians must have played it several times together, gone over certain passages, agreed on the tempo. Therefore it is probable that this violinist and pianist have not played it before because they are struck dumb at some moment by the music — it is a surprise to them. If they had practiced it they would be concentrating on giving a good performance this time, getting the crescendo right, increasing the fortissimo.

In the Brahms D Minor the great climax comes in the third movement. They have therefore already played two movements together. This means that one is in a high state of irritation at the other because one artist always does play a little better or let us say a little differently from another. In the picture the violinist looks shabby, he suggests a professor or perhaps a teacher. He is I think the professional and the lady is the amateur. At the climax I believe the violinist wants to take his bow and hit her over the head with it because she is not in time and can't keep up. At that moment he hates her.

I have never known a musician to be late for a professional engagement. He is in the greenroom nervously pacing up and down a good forty minutes before the concert begins. He may dress in an individual style but it is carefully thought out. He is well aware of the hundreds of eyes that are studying his cutaway or dress suit. His attire is not careless.

The artists who tour America, who gave concerts in Europe before the war, can remember in a moment what are the seating capacities of the various halls and opera houses from Munich to San Francisco. They know the gross, they understand the per cent. Managers may grow nostalgic for the dreamy artist who does not understand about money, but he seldom has the pleasure of dealing with one.

My father once asked Rachmaninoff what he was really looking at when he gazed at the gallery with that tiger stare which so fascinated and frightened audiences.

"Counting the standees in the balcony," said Rachmaninoff. "The manager told me they were not allowed, but there were forty-three."

If artists live in studios, they also live in apartments, suburban houses, bungalows. There is a hotel in New York on the West Side which is one of the ugliest hotels in the world. It has a gargantuan lobby in picked metal, its corridors stretch endlessly, the rooms have golden chandeliers full of bright electric bulbs. Here live some of our greatest musicians. The manager loves music. He knows about late suppers and later breakfasts. He keeps the rooms for the tenor who is touring in South America. He has a bouquet of red roses waiting for him with "Welcome Home" written on it. There are no pastel colors on the walls, no candlelight, but the most beautiful music played today is played in that hotel.

What is the special quality that differentiates the musician from the sculptor, the painter, the writer? To me it lies in the fact that he so loves his art that he pursues it not only as a profession but also for relaxation. He makes his career in music, and then has not had enough of it; he makes his gaiety and good times with music also. Heifetz and Casals will play in a Mozart quartet — for fun. Melchior will sing a big role in the opera, but will sing German lieder for the general joy of a group of friends — and himself. Watch a musician staying at a house where there is no piano. He may not want to play the piano but it ought to be there. He feels lonely and insecure without it.

A trait that musicians share is their love of good food. No one ever had a poor meal in a musician's home. The artists who travel so much and so far learn very quickly which are the good restaurants in the different cities. After a performance they eat with zest and they eat well. They are relaxed and the moment comes for the stories to be exchanged. In their travels musicians hear the good jokes from all over the world and it is a sort of unwritten law that when they return to base they will exchange with brother artists the latest anecdotes.

Paul Kochanski was one of the greatest of raconteurs. Acting out the characters, using four languages, mimicking the voices, interpolating with his violin, he would keep a roomful of people crying with laughter. His eye and ear missed nothing. In the presence of Spalding and Heifetz and Zimbalist he would imitate their individual way of playing the same passage and taking a curtain call, a satire which they were the first to recognize and laugh over.

And later in the evening with Artur Rubinstein, Paul played the César Franck Sonata in a way which brought other tears to the eyes of the little audience crowded on chairs and sitting on the floor; moved beyond words at this perfect example of the creative something that the great interpretive musicians bring to music. Paul and Artur played César Franck, but in the poetry of their playing was the essence of themselves.

As far back as I can remember my sisters and I heard music in our home. We had our favorites among the musicians but not because of their particular artistic merit. Our praise and admiration went to those who remembered our names individually and did not speak of us as "the little daughters," to those who brought us presents, and above all to those who were funny. This was to us the supreme test of musical worth. We sat with the men over their cigars, slightly concealed by a portiere, so that we could watch the expressive face of Ossip Gabrilowitsch as he told my father an anecdote, and then tried to hide our shrieks of amusement in the general masculine roar. We peered at Alma Gluck from behind a screen not just because she was so beautiful but because she was the only woman we knew who could tell a story as well as a man.

There was another side to knowing the artists which we did not always enjoy, in fact which we frequently protested against. My father would invite to the house some musician whom he had met in Europe or who was to perform with the orchestra, and he did not always know the artist well. The violinist would come with his wife, the singer with her husband, and we would be left to entertain the consort. My father could never be clear to us as to what the consort was like. The words "charming" and "original" were used frequently but often, we felt, inaccurately.

One day my father announced quite suddenly that Monsieur Aragonnes, leading French clarinet player of the Colonne Orchestra, was coming to lunch with his wife and that they were bringing their child. Now here my father made that unforgivable error of not realizing that ages are different. All between five and sixteen were children to him and should get on harmoniously together. Though we pointed out again and again the vast gap that existed between say eleven and thirteen, he could not grasp it and continued to invite what were to us incongruous specimens of childhood.

We gathered in the living room before lunch and waited in utter cynicism for Monsieur and Madame Aragonnes and the "child." My father had no idea of its sex.

"What difference does it make!" he exclaimed.

First Monsieur entered, smiling happily at seeing my father again. Then came Madame, dressed in a black suit with a white satin blouse, black hat with an aigrette, face beautifully made up, gleaming teeth, and snapping black eyes. Following them came the child. He was a youth of about seventeen, with the shadowy feather of a mustache on his upper lips, an adolescent complexion, and possessing faultless and to us revolting manners.

"Chère Madame," said Monsieur Aragonnes after he had presented his wife to my mother, "voilà notre jeune fils, notre petit garçon, Pépé."

So, Monsieur made the same mistake as my father by referring to his aged son as a little boy. Perhaps we had a bond with him there. We looked at him hopefully. Not a gleam in his eye — Pépé liked it!

"Madame," and Pépé bowed low over my mother's hand as he kissed it. "Mademoiselles — " he went to each of us and shook our hands. At the final "Mademoiselle" his voice took on a different color. Could he be patronizing *us* because he thought he was so sophisticated?

At luncheon Pépé entered into the conversation as an equal. He discussed the performance of *Istar* by Vincent d'Indy. Had my father played the latest work of Ducasse? *Très intéressant*. We listened to him with hatred. He was supposed to be our friend. We didn't want him in that role but we wanted — a little recognition. How affected he was to speak French so well. And his English — like an Englishman. What a show-off.

After lunch my father retired to his music room with

Monsieur, his clarinet, a roll of music, and Madame who was to accompany her husband. My mother went upstairs. We were left with Pépé.

Now here we were faced with several choices. To try to humiliate Pépé and make him come down off his high horse; to try to impress him how much better Americans were than Frenchmen; to start talking an invented language to each other and tell him it was Hungarian; to inform him falsely of the customs of our country, or to give him one more chance. We could avail ourselves of none of these possibilities. Pépé took charge of the conversation.

Did we go to school? No, French boys went to the lycée, much more difficult, like an American college. His hair had fallen out on one side of his head during the last examinations. What instruments did we play? Of course everyone played the piano but he was majoring in the viola and played the flute for relaxation. Had we been often to Paris? That was unfortunate as it was the most beautiful city in the world; did we know it was called the city of light? For sport he preferred fencing and mountain climbing, he had made the ascent of Mt. Blanc only last summer.

We closed in on him.

"Pépé, have you seen Buffalo Bill yet? You don't know what we are talking about! Which do you think is

funnier, Foxy Grandpa or the Katzenjammer Kids?
You've never tasted a Banana Split? You've never seen
a minstrel show? You don't know what the loop-the-
loop is? In a minute you'll tell us you have never heard
of Uncle Tom!"

We looked at each other in exaggerated surprise. We
looked at Pépé with ostentatious pity.

"Why, you must have spent your whole life in Paris!"

Pépé's face turned pink. At this moment the clarinet
in the next room let off an unearthly wail which ended
in a kind of shriek. All our eyes met. Pépé's face turned
red. He walked over to the door and slammed it.

"Je déteste Fauré et plus que ça, je déteste la cla-
rinette!"

We looked at him with surprised admiration. How
bold to bang the door on your father. And then Pépé's
eyes abruptly filled with real tears. We were in con-
sternation.

Polly ran out of the room and brought down her alligator John D. Crockefeller and let Pépé hold it. We
examined the thinner side of Pépé's head and told him
we thought French schools were brutal. We confessed
we hated practicing the piano. We extended condo-
lences to him for being called such a silly name as Pépé.
We told him we thought his mother looked nice and he
said she was difficult in the early morning. We advised

him to give up kissing hands. We wound up the gramophone.

Monsieur and Madame Aragonnes entered the room with my father.

"Ah, la jeunesse, la jeunesse," cried Monsieur as Madame smoothed the thicker side of Pépé's head. We tried to encourage Pépé by our looks.

"You see," said my father after they had gone, "how foolish you are to object when a nice French boy comes to lunch."

We didn't even attempt to explain that he was not nice until we had made him so by our Old World courtesy.

We were excited when we were told Brünnhilde was coming to the house. Brünnhilde who had been ringed by fire, awakened by Siegfried, was coming to a meal. My father said she might sing on the spring tour with the orchestra if certain details could be ironed out.

She arrived without her shield and spear, but with her husband. She was large, that we knew for we had seen her in the opera, but it was a different kind of largeness in Tyroler tweeds. We thought of her as a goddess, above all earthly needs, but now this daughter of Wotan was eating a big lunch with amazing gusto, telling about her *Kinder* in Dresden, informing my mother that *bei uns* politics is the man's business, *der Liebe Gott* intended women for better things, assuring my father that Pol Plançon, the great French bass, flattened in his upper register and was finished.

My father protested that this was not true.

"Ach, I could tell you a thing or two about the Opera. There should be many changes there. Take Sembrich — "

"I'll take her anywhere," cried my father. "I adore her."

Brünnhilde's eyes flashed. For a moment she looked again like a real Valkyrie. We waited breathless for a glorious note to be hurled across the table.

"If Sembrich had a private car for her tour, I too must have a private car!"

"*Schatzchen*, do not excite yourself," begged her husband who had been listening with a nervous smile. He turned to my father. "She is only a child. She must save her strength for her exhausting roles. She must not concern herself with business arrangements. Leave them to me."

"If Sembrich had a private car — " repeated Brünnhilde.

"Eat another *Kuchen*," urged her husband. "*Echte Viener Torte*." He turned to my mother. "I congratulate you."

"I didn't bake it!" exclaimed my mother, still seething over the description of God's intentions for women.

Brünnhilde ate another slice of cake and said she had no appetite.

"Damrosch, let us be frank. Let us have no misunderstandings. I admire you, I like you. We are friends — yes?"

"Yes," said my father.

"This is between us. The Bruno, my husband, is a businessman, so he cannot understand the strain that a dramatic soprano who sings twenty-seven roles works under. The good Mrs. Damrosch is a wife, a mother, the noblest of all careers, but she cannot realize what it is to conduct a great orchestra. You and I — we are artists. We know what that means!"

"What does it mean?" asked my father.

"It means," announced Brünnhilde in a loud voice, "that if Sembrich had a private car, I too will have a private car!"

My father remained unperturbed.

"Tell me," he said, "why have you never sung Eva?"

"Never sung Eva! Tell him, Bruno, in Vienna, at Stockholm, at the Hamburg Municipal Theater — the ovations!"

"Then why not in New York?"

"Because they do not know what makes a good *Meis-*

tersinger in New York! They have never heard a real Eva."

"How would it be," suggested my father, "if on the tour we gave some excerpts from the second act?"

Brünnhilde's face was suddenly illuminated by a brilliant smile.

"Ah, that is a great idea! Damrosch, I do not care what anyone else says, you are a genius! Come let me show you. Where is the piano?"

"You have eaten a large lunch," reminded Bruno.

"I ate nothing. Where is the piano?"

Bruno, my mother, and the rest of us sat on in the dining room. Bruno looked at my mother a little wanly.

"She is like a child," he repeated, without much conviction.

At that moment we did not care what she was, we knew it had no importance. Whatever she asked for she should be given. For with the first great chords of music we heard her voice. Our home had become a garden in old Nuremberg bathed in moonlight, and Eva was stealing out from the shadows toward Hans Sachs. We listened, spellbound.

Watching the consorts I used to wonder what their contribution was. The men in this role I did not think fared so well. Their queens bore a different name, made a great deal of money all over the world, often felt victimized and needed their husbands to straighten out their difficulties and above all to reassure them. This historically is the role of woman. It is not an easy part for a man to play. Sometimes a great singer was married to a gambler and was feverishly trying to put aside enough to pay his debts. He was the love of her life and he was unfaithful to her. But the Daemon that possesses the artist world never has allowed her to give up her career and stay with him.

This Daemon, this thing in the artist, is the chemistry of his make-up. Women have always liked to feel that they can inspire, that they can cause the great notes to be written. As I observed the variety of consorts who came to our home I found I did not believe this. One wife might make the right atmosphere, produce the protected quiet, but another did just the opposite. She was loud-mouthed and self-centered. An artist married to the woman who built up his ego and produced the sympathetic circle of admirers and patrons undoubtedly made life pleasanter for her husband. But there was the opposite picture of the artist's wife who made enemies and had taken to drink. And her husband was the bigger musician.

He was big — because he was big; because somehow the Daemon had entered his being and ruled him, beside which his wife, his children, the right atmosphere, the beautiful background, were as nothing. He served something else which was much stronger, which demanded creation from him. The rest could help or hinder — a little.

Women must feel necessary; they seem happiest when they feel used. The artist's wife and the wife of the brakeman have that in common. The artist is more prominent so his wife's role is subjected to a brighter light of observation, but both wives are I believe giving the identical contribution — the companion who stands between, who reassures, who is there.

I used to feel sorry for some of the wives who were touring with their husbands. They were so very far from home and so homesick for their children. Sooner or later they would bring out their snapshots to show my mother. Then with a little urging they would show us further pictures of their homes in Switzerland or in France — such pretty homes which they would not see for many months.

The day that Paderewski came to lunch we had excuses to leave school early. My mother had taken great trouble in ordering the food. We had at this time a German chef called Karl who preferred cooking for occasions. At six in the morning he was already hard at work. Karl wanted to show Paderewski the kind of performance he could give.

My sisters and I knew we would get a wonderful lunch but let it be said to our credit we were more excited at the prospect of watching Paderewski eat. We had met him, we had heard him play, but we had never seen him eat. Madame Paderewska had asked that there be no other guests so we knew that no matter where we were placed at table we would have an uninterrupted view of the hands of Paderewski lifting the fork of Paderewski to the mouth of Paderewski through four long courses.

What was the quality that made him so frightening when he entered the room? He was so individual looking in his frock coat, low white collar, and white tie, with his great head of reddish hair, his long arms, his beautiful hands; but it was his eyes that were so extraordinary. They had the remote look and the hidden fire of a wild animal; they looked as though they had seen things that no one had ever seen before. They suggested that Paderewski had not come from Poland, but was from a distant planet where the race was even older, wiser. And he had such dignity that one would not have dared say or do anything that could disturb him. He spoke in a soft voice but the quality of the tone could silence a room in a second. Paderewski had great wit and could cap anyone, but it was a little like a god disguising himself for a moment as a mortal before he withdrew again to Olympus.

Madame Paderewska seemed surrounded by an aura of melancholy. I do not know if it was anxiety for her famous husband, or her temperament, but her quality was depressing. She meant to be cordial but it was a very gloomy kind of good cheer. If Paderewski threw back his head and laughed I felt that Madame Paderewska's main concern was a fear that he might strain his neck muscles. She watched him with such a troubled look. She did not speak English well and when the conversation became rapid she may have felt excluded.

The first course came on the table and we saw that Karl had outdone himself. We waited, careful not to start eating until the Paderewskis ate. He was talking to my father. We waited a little longer; then Madame Paderewska spoke.

"Madame Damrosch, pliz, may Ignace have a poached egg?"

"What!" exclaimed my father.

"Ignace for luncheon only eats an egg."

"But this is a simple dish," said my father falsely, "I know he will enjoy it."

"Pliz, an egg," repeated Madame Paderewska firmly. "Nossing else."

My mother commanded the egg. We heard the dumb-waiter bell buzz and the order being hissed down to Karl. We were all of us distractedly picturing the scene below. Karl's spirit would be broken. Could he pull himself together enough to poach the egg? Would it come up — just an egg — or might he make the supreme effort and put it on a little piece of toast and trim it up with parsley?

Paderewski had withdrawn to his mountain top. I wondered what that faraway look in his eyes meant. My father had told us how much he enjoyed good food. I became convinced he wanted to eat everything we were eating. He was off there on that mountain because he was mad.

In the middle of the second course the dumb-waiter creaked again and the eggs arrived, two of them, on toast, with fixings. Lunch became lively, Paderewski's eyes lighted, and wherever he had been, he left it and joined the party again.

Later we watched the Paderewskis through the window as they left. He was wearing a round fur cap on top of his waving hair. Madame Paderewska hung onto his arm and people turned to stare as they walked slowly up the street. My mother and father went down to the kitchen to face Karl.

Isadora Duncan had no consort. She came unheralded to New York, this strange little California genius who was to change the conception of the Dance for many years. My father went to see her in an old loft downtown; she was too poor to have a proper studio. She danced in front of some gray curtains which had been tacked up as a background. My father was struck dumb by the simple figure in its Greek kirtle who moved so joyously to the music of Schubert. It was a Tanagra figure come alive again. He recognized her wonderful art, took the gamble, and engaged her at his own risk to dance with the orchestra. This was a bold move on his part for great orchestras were not supposed to perform with dancers. But Isadora made a furore and the public, accustomed to the artificial ballet on the toes, went wild with delight at this new old form.

I was very young when I saw her but I remember that I cried — my first tears shed at the startling quality of beauty. I must have been studying mythology for it seemed to me that Isadora was Daphne dancing in some ancient glade, and that behind the trees lurked Apollo, but that she, the nymph, did not know or care if he was there. Let him later transform her to a laurel, but now she wanted only to dance alone to the music of Gluck, a wild and happy creature — for she was free.

I went to every performance of Isadora that my parents allowed me and of course decided that I could dance that way too. It was so simple; that was its essence. Secretly I went to Bloomingdale's big department store and bought cheesecloth for a costume. It was very cheap, eleven cents a yard, and I wanted to be sure I had enough, so I bought a bolt, enough to outfit a hundred Greeks in kirtles. When it arrived I found it was of double width and I did not know how to cut it out. I made a hole for my head, sewed up the sides, chopped off the bottom, and tied the corded belt of my wrapper around my waist. The part over my shoulders was so wide that it dropped down over my hands every time I made a whirl with my arms, but I did not dare ask the advice of Minnie or my sisters for I knew that they would laugh at me.

I performed in Alice's room when she was out because it gave me more space and because she had a mirror on her bureau which could be tilted, so that when I floated out of her closet door, for a brief second I could see myself in entirety from bare Greek feet to flower-covered Greek head.

I was completely happy — not that I felt I was beginning a career which would shortly lead me to Carnegie Hall; I had no such ambition because I was too humble and some inner voice told me I was a gawk. I wanted to recapture for myself the thrill of joy I had felt in watching Isadora, and in this I succeeded. Alice's room became a Delphic grove and thanks to the fact that the mirror could only reflect bits of me, I was a dryad and my humming voice an orchestra.

Isadora Duncan as an artist had genius, as a person she was a goose. It must have been a God-given instinct which was infallible when she created the form of her dances; there was a rightness about all of them. But when she talked she was almost idiotic. She had theories about everything and my father had to listen to all of them.

He would watch her across the footlights, enraptured, and then she would come to the house and he and my mother would become rapidly unenraptured, almost frantic. Isadora admired my father and was grateful to him for giving her her start and I think felt that in return she should liberate him. She was very concerned over "freedom" and felt that everyone must strive for it. But it was difficult in our house to free my father. There was my mother and there were his daughters always sitting around. There never seemed to be the right moment to break his chains.

She called my father "Walter" and my mother "Mrs. Damrosch" and still my father remained tied. She urged my father to come to her chilly loft after a performance to really talk about fundamentals but my father said he was hot from conducting and wanted to get home and take a bath. So Isadora had to come to our home to explain to my father in her curiously flat little voice how one should live if one really wanted to live.

She would appear in a velvet cloak and Victorian bonnet, the costume that she affected during the daytime, and my mother, who greatly admired her dancing, would praise her latest performance to the skies. Isadora would thank my mother graciously and then ask if a lamp or two could be turned out because she could express herself better in a dim light.

Whether my mother was there or not, I sat happily with my father and Isadora. It never crossed my mind that such a true adorer of her art as myself could be anything but gratifying to her. I do not think that my father noticed one way or the other. He was too used to seeing his daughters about. But now in retrospect I can imagine that to have your great conclusions on Life, intended for a kindred spirit but listened to so eagerly by a twelve-year-old in a plaid skirt and red sweater on which was embroidered an "H" for Harvard, must have been to Isadora a ghastly comeuppance.

Because I helped the conversation along. Whenever there was a pause, a silent, significant pause in the dim light, I filled it in. A silence I knew very well meant that no one could think of anything to say and was embarrassing, so I added my observations to cover up the gaps.

I remember that one afternoon Isadora started to tell my father about Venice; that she was returning to that glorious city because she wanted again to find herself. She would be alone . . . perhaps . . .

There was a pause.

"Oh, I'd like to see Venice," I piped up. "Can't we all go next summer, Parp?"

There was a slightly longer pause.

"My child," said Isadora finally, "you will go to Venice some day — with someone. I see you have that capacity. But I want you to remember what I am telling you. When you go, love beautifully. That is all that ever matters."

This was strong meat. I chewed it over. I couldn't get it out of my head. Isadora saw me so to speak as potential Venetian material. I floated off in a cloud.

But later I found Jenny dusting the piano with one of my Greek costumes. I came back to earth with a bang.

(14)

All Aboard — Toot, Toot

A T THE end of August older people had a way of talking as if the summer were over. They talked about railroad tickets when the leaves were still green. They talked about an obscure date called "when school opens."

Minnie liked trunks in rooms weeks before they had to be used, and she loved keys. She never threw any away and she never marked them but kept them by the hundreds in a big tin box. This meant she had to sit on the floor and try them in the locks for days and days. My mother liked to throw things out relentlessly, so valuable articles had to be concealed from her if she didn't happen to understand their use. My father became bowed down over the problems of how to pack his music with his shoes. And all this restless confusion was caused because there had been a couple of cold nights, because the goldenrod had appeared along the roadsides.

But this year my mother and Minnie were left undisturbed to throw out and hoard, because all of us were getting ready for a big event. We were preparing for the annual Pop Concert.

The Pop Concert was given in a hall called the Casino or the library depending on which door was used in the daytime. For several summers a part of the entertainment was provided by our family and the Sherwood family who lived further up Lake Champlain. The Sherwood part of the entertainment was dominated by their youngest son, called Bobby.

This year Mrs. Sherwood and my father had pooled their talents for an act, leaving Bobby as usual to do his part in his own way, undisputed. To have Mrs. Sherwood in our camp was an enormous advantage to us for she was an artist belonging to that brilliant family of Emmets where the gift of painting has been passed on to the women of the family through many generations. The strain runs only in the females of the line. I am told that in Emmet attics there are huge oil canvases painted by Emmet ladies of the eighteenth century when nice women were supposed to sketch a little with crayons.

My father had planned as an episode in some sort of charade a pantomime of "Bluebeard" for which he was creating the music. My Aunt H. was to direct it if she could keep my father from interfering too much — a highly doubtful possibility — and Mrs. Sherwood was designing the *décors* and generally supervising the costumes, make-up, and lighting effects. The climax was to occur when the little wife of Bluebeard entered through the forbidden door. Here Mrs. Sherwood had painted a miraculous backdrop and had cut some holes in it on different levels through which the real heads of the unhappy wives were to appear apparently hung by their hair as blood dripped down from their necks. Mrs. Sherwood planned to make up the faces with a deathly pallor and my father had composed some very ghostly music.

I was to be a head and my instructions were to keep my eyes shut and my face composed. I was quite satisfied with the part, it seemed to me a good one, until rumors began to reach me about Bobby's end of the show. It sounded as though this summer there were going to be even more "production" in it than usual. I suddenly wanted to be in on his scene. It was all very well to be in a pantomime with a sister or two, my cousin Walker and his friends, and my same old father at the piano, but the "Act, composed, written, directed and produced by Robert Emmet Sherwood" would have all the class. I would be in that section of the entertainment which would be described by those hated words, "So very artistic," but Bobby's part I knew very well would be hailed as "Hot Stuff, oh boy!"

Bobby was about thirteen years old when he reached the full flower of his creative genius. He was just twice as tall as any of his contemporaries. He began doubling on their height when he was a small boy and he kept to his record in manhood. His mother cut the ends off his sneakers so he could fit into them and still he kept on growing.

Bobby always had great conceptual plans for his productions. He brooded alone and dreamed his dreams which must have been clear to him, but he never wrote a scene down or explained clearly to his cast what he expected of them. If he saw a drama perfect and whole in his head, it was unbelievable to him that a few muttered words through his nose in the way of plot, dialogue, and direction would not immediately create a snappy and sparkling scene. He would become indignant, then furious. He would give up in despair and look elsewhere for actors who weren't so dumb.

His mother seemed to grasp at times what Bobby was after and would help him. She painted the scenery that she thought he intended, she cut out masks and sewed costumes and tried out lighting effects. She listened to his ideas, apparently found a clue or two, and went ahead.

There was one actress whom Bobby believed in and with whom he almost co-starred, or at least allowed to hold the position of leading lady. This was Mrs. James Still, the Sherwood cook. Mrs. Still had two great advantages. She did exactly what Bobby told her to do without argument, and she could play the banjo. In her Bobby finally found his perfect foil and gradually his acts became exclusively himself and Mrs. Still as a team, with an occasional chorus which was allowed to appear briefly for the finale.

Mrs. Still played nearly all her roles in blackface and her main assignment, besides the banjo, was to feed Bobby lines. Bobby never gave her the speeches with the laughs. Those he kept for himself. Bobby played in black or white and was usually the sporting type, wearing his brother's long white trousers, a checked jacket, a striped tie, and a natty stiff straw hat which he lifted from his head and held at an angle as he did his exit buck and wing. He always carried a cane. He never smiled, he was a very serious actor, but his distraught, almost agonized face, as he performed, always produced the desired effect. He brought down the house.

Mrs. Sherwood had been using me as a model for two water colors that she was painting. I found it curiously pleasant to sit in her garden holding a basket of fruit as

I gazed into space. I felt occupied and important and yet I had nothing to do but to dream along in a peaceful stupor as I looked out over the garden to the lawns and lake beyond. I saw Bobby in the distance chopping down a large tree.

"Bobby is chopping down one of your best trees," I told Mrs. Sherwood.

"It's for a scene; I don't quite know what the tree is going to be but it's not going to be a tree."

We both of us nodded and I was again impressed and jealous. I could make a scene with sheets but it had never occurred to me to cut down one of my father's trees. There was no getting away from it — Bobby did things in a big way.

"Is the tree going to lie down?" I asked.

"Not at first," said Mrs. Sherwood, "but I imagine it will fall down."

"What do you think he thinks the tree will be?"

"A tower, a crocodile — a staircase; how can I tell?"

"I suppose it will be in his scene at the Pop Concert, won't it?" I asked wistfully.

Mrs. Sherwood did not answer. It was a secret.

The tree crashed and we both turned. Bobby was approaching an even larger one with his axe.

"You can't have that one!" cried his mother gesticulating at him. "Move up there. Take one in the woods."

Bobby looked up indignantly.

"This is the one I've got to have!"

"No, no!" shouted Mrs. Sherwood. "That's my biggest maple. You can't have it!"

Sulkily Bobby withdrew up the hill and Mrs. Sherwood returned to her picture. I watched her as she painted and thought how concentrated she was and how handsome. That was the way I would like to be when I grew older. I tried to make my face very beautiful.

"Don't look so gloomy," said Mrs. Sherwood. "You're sagging everywhere. Think of something else."

I attempted to rearrange my features more cheerfully but still along lovely lines.

"Never mind," said Mrs. Sherwood after a moment in a kindly tone. "I only need the figure as a foreground for my hollyhocks."

We sat silent for a few minutes and then I saw her in what I believed to be a slow suicide. She was sucking the paint off her brushes. The inside of her mouth was green and brown and at the moment she was squeezing a tube of yellow onto her palette.

"Let me get you some more water!" I exclaimed.

"Don't change your pose," ordered Mrs. Sherwood.

Minnie had warned us often that paint was poison. Had no one ever told Mrs. Sherwood? I must stop her.

"Don't you know you'll die if you eat paint!"

"I've always sucked my brushes," said Mrs. Sherwood, "and I always shall."

I was deeply moved. What a strange way for her to end — poisoned in her own garden. I gazed at her sorrowfully. I liked her so very much. Mrs. Sherwood sucked some yellow off the brush. I began to get kind of excited. Would she fall off her chair suddenly? Would she scream?

Mrs. Sherwood is now ninety-one years old.

I walked home the four miles and pondered over the Pop Concert. Bobby was difficult; one couldn't just say to him, "I want to be in your act." I didn't identify the feeling with as lofty a word as "pride," but I wanted to be wanted for my talents. And he hadn't asked me. If I forced it, I might get a bad surprise. The year before Bobby had given a circus and his little sister Rosamond had insisted that she be in it. I had never been sure that she was given a good role. Rosamond had been drawn around in a small cart on which was written, "The Mother of All the Freaks."

When I reached home I received my bad surprise. Polly told me in a "by the way" manner which I found peculiarly irritating that she had transferred to Bobby's act. She was not going to be "just an old head." She was going to wear a costume — and sing. I tried to find out further details.

"It's a secret," said Polly.

We rehearsed the pantomime and my father and my Aunt H. had many fiery disputes over what were the appropriate gestures to express certain emotions.

"This is the way to show horror," said my father, raising his arms to the heavens.

"No! No!" exclaimed Aunt H. "It's like this," and she clutched at her throat and then hid her face.

"Are you trying to teach an old hand like me!" asked my father in the voice of David Belasco.

"I look at you, Walter," said my aunt, "I hear what you say — I am horrified — like this!" and she clutched her throat again.

"It should be one simple gesture — like this," and my father raised his arms.

"Go back to your music," begged Aunt H.

The cast waited patiently in a long row, eating popcorn. We knew of old that the arguments always took just twice as long as the acting.

"Now we will start again from the moment Bluebeard enters and gives Fatima the keys," said Aunt H., swiftly trying to establish her authority. "Ready, Walter?"

The scene was played again to the moment of horror. My father turned around to watch. My cousin Walker grabbed at another boy's throat and he retaliated fiercely. My father improvised a faster accompaniment.

"I think that's rather good, H.," he commented.

"What did I tell you," said my aunt triumphantly.

My mother sat in the front row with Minnie. Through the hall were scattered other parents, friends, guests from the Inn, and two rows of the boys from Camp Dudley. Camp Dudley was fourteen miles away, almost in another county it took so long to drive there, and was famous for its minstrel shows. The boys of Camp Dudley were known to be ferocious critics. The cast fought for the hole in the curtain to study them and their mood for the evening. There was that pleasant queasy feeling in all stomachs. Mrs. Sherwood sat in a dressing room applying pallor to the wives' faces.

The lights were lowered and on the curtain appeared a series of pictures from a jack-o'-lantern, displaying Harry Braman, Fine Meats; A. B. Blinn, Dealers in Everything; The Westport National Bank; The Inn, Golf, Tennis, and Summer Fun. Each of the pictures received applause until that of the Inn appeared, when Camp Dudley whistled piercingly and sarcastically. Westport responded with louder enthusiasm. The final picture showed George E. Richards Drugstore which was given a great and defiant ovation, but it was apparent that the audience was aligning itself into opposing loyalties. The Bluebeard Company began to get very nervous. Would Dudley accept a pantomime?

My father sat down at the piano, was received courteously by both groups, the curtain started up, wouldn't roll, came down again, there were some audible suggestions from the wings, the curtain rose again, jerkily, and "Bluebeard" opened.

Fortunately in a pantomime there are no lines to be forgotten. And you cannot be prompted. The cues are in the music, and if an actor misses, it is up to the music to follow and get things straightened out again. My father may have been startled at the speed with which the stark tragedy was enacted, and how often certain passages that he had so lovingly conceived were jumped, but he kept valiantly along and improvised when there was a confusion in the cast as to the next move.

The audience was attentive and quiet but there was no real indication of their feelings. Then came a pale bluish light on the stage and Fatima was confronted by the white faces of the slain wives, hanging by their hair. Mrs. Sherwood had done a great and gory job. The heads were very, very dead.

There was an audible gasp from the public and sud-

denly an intoxicating sound filled the hall — applause.
I forgot my instructions. I opened my eyes and looked.
I wanted to see what Camp Dudley thought about it.
Camp Dudley was not clapping — but also it was not
whistling. For the pantomimists, this was their minor
triumph.

For the Sherwood Act the Bluebeard Company sat
in the back of the house along the window sills. A new
pianist took the place of my father — Earl Braman,
son of Harry Braman, Fine Meats. He was augmented
by a drummer. An expectant hush came over the audience. Camp Dudley leaned forward. This was their
challenge.

The music opened with an introduction and then
went into a vamp. The vamp was played twice and the
curtain rose — smoothly — on a front drop of a street
scene. A Negro porter entered, carrying a bag. He was
played by Huger Labouisse, a boy from New Orleans
considered an authority on the Southern accent. He
was followed by Mrs. Still, also in blackface and carrying her banjo. Huger Labouisse and Mrs. Still were apparently husband and wife and she was grieving that he
must leave her again and go on another journey. During the vamp they discussed this with a series of remark-
ably sophisticated jokes on marriage which were greeted
uproariously by the younger members of the audience.

The vamp grew louder, the drum joined in with a couple of rolls, a voice off stage called "Porter, porter!" Mrs. Still began to strum softly on her banjo, and Robert Sherwood entered, wearing white trousers, checked jacket, striped tie, stiff straw hat, and carrying a cane. He ignored the waves of applause, and turning fiercely to the porter asked him why he was so slow, and to shuffle along.

"Where you goin', Massa?" cried Mrs. Still.

Bobby turned toward the audience, leaning slightly on his cane, and with a tortured look on his face sang: —

I've had a mighty busy day —
I've had to pack my things away,
Now I'm going to give the landlord back his key —
The very key that opened up my dreary flat
Where many weary nights I sat,
Thinking of the folks down home who think of me,
. . . You can bet you'll find me sing-ing hap-pi-ly —

Mrs. Still here played her banjo with full force.

When the midnight choo-choo leaves for Alabam' —
I'll be right there —
I've got my fare.
When I see that rusty haired conductor-man,
I'll grab him by the collar
And I'll holler
"Al-a-bam'! Al-a-bam'!"

Bobby now started pacing up and down as he sang with greater violence at the audience: —

> That's where you stop your train —
> That brings me back again, —
> Down home where I'll remain —
> Where my hon-ey lamb
> Am.
> I will be right there with bells —
> When that old con-duc-tor yells, —
> All a-board! (toot toot)
> All a-board! (toot toot)
> All a-board for Al-a-bam'!

The great climax came at the conclusion of the chorus. The street-scene curtain rose.

How does a mother feel when she first looks upon her baby? What were Colonel Goethals's emotions when he first gazed upon the completed Panama Canal? On the stage left stood an actual, built and painted train and through its actual windows peered a large and brilliantly dressed group of passengers who sang in almost too close harmony: —

> When that midnight choo-choo leaves for Alabam' —
> I'll be right there—
> I've got my fare.

But this was not all. The lights on the stage blacked out, real lights appeared in the car windows (made by flashlights held by the passengers), and as the chorus was repeated pianissimo, the train *moved* across the stage.

As it neared the exit, Bobby and the porter carrying his bag jumped on, and Bobby, holding his hat at an angle, sang alone at the top of his lungs, from the end of the car: —

> I will be right there with bells —
> When that old con-duc-tor yells, —
> All a-board! — (toot toot)
> All a-board! — (toot toot)

Here Earl Braman blew a real train whistle: —

> All a-board for Al-a-bam'!

I was not present at the premier of *Aïda* but I imagine it created the same furore. Camp Dudley recognized the touch of the master. This was Production. They gave it the great tribute — they pounded with their feet. Hot Stuff. Oh Boy!

End of Summer

THERE was red on the hills and red in the swamps. There was that unmistakable warning, "It is ending, it is about to begin." It was as though there were a choice in the still, smoky air — as though one were on a springboard and could leap to an older age or by some magic hold onto it, this happy time, this Indian summer.

Children feel it, animals feel it as they stretch out in the sun together and watch the yellow leaves float by. They cling to each other for deeply they hear a drumbeat in the air, and the rhythm of the beat is saying, "Things don't last."

Walker with his friend Blair Lee lay with us on the grass. Beside them sat Punk, Walker's dog, agonizedly looking at them. Punk didn't need the bags to tell him they were leaving tomorrow for school. He read the calendar on my aunt's desk and saw the circle round the date.

All of us were wishing at this moment that the clock would stop and our parents would stop planning and talking about what was to come. Though we had talked and planned boldly too, as the day drew near we were secretly filled with anxiety and apprehension. One never could be sure that after the lapse of time one's friends would still like one. And there was that problem which weighed like the world on an Atlas — one must be older, or make others think that one had aged.

And today, this last day, none of us wanted to be reminded of these things. Instead we wanted to be captains of our fate once more, to be tyrants over the young, to own the hours and spend them as we liked. We searched for an escape from our insecurity and we couldn't find the key. We needed to conjure up a genie who would pour Dutch courage down our throats, thump us on the backs and give us again our sense of power. But we didn't know the spell.

Rama, the sheep dog, came slowly across the grass. He was very, very old. He was feeble yet no other dog dared draw near him when he growled. He still lumbered a little way into the lake, he still buried his bones, he still laughed when we laughed, but he moaned in his sleep at night and a remoteness had come over him.

It was as though he had started on his journey to the next place and then had turned around to see if we wouldn't come too so that he need not go alone.

I put my arms about him and hugged him. Then like a superstition he became to me the symbol of the genie and I made a bargain with my fate. While Rama was there I need not be frightened of any future because he did not expect any more of me than what I was — I could in very truth be my age. But if anything happened to Rama, irrevocably this thing — I suppose I meant my youth — would go with him, and my world, the world to which all evidence pointed that I was the center, would smash.

Somehow comforted by this strange compact I turned and squinted at the blue water. It was so still, so warm, one could pretend it was July. But in my heart I knew the summer hush was counterfeit.

My mother suggested a farewell picnic for the boys, supper up the lake.

Picnics are historically our great link with the past. They never vary much. Look at a Renoir, an earlier Fragonard. There is the same effort of a group to find "the beauty spot." There is the lady with the extra shawl, the man who has opened his shirt front to the sun. There is the boy who lies easily on the ground, the older gentleman who rests with obvious discomfort against a tree. There are the same baskets of food; the same slight mess everywhere.

The scenes are so similar that one may presume that the feelings of the picnickers also have not altered. The ladies have seized this chance for a day outdoors, a day to escape from fussing about a meal at home. They love it. The men in varying degrees hate it. It is the great sex divergence. Women arrange picnics joyfully — men go protestingly. They would rather sit comfortably at home, or go and climb a mountain and then come home, or sail a boat, but always come home to eat. Most men have been broken in over the years, and they go. They cannot resist the age-old pressure. In their inheritance is a fiber, weakened through centuries, that cannot withstand this battle call to a picnic.

I believe that the men's last great stand took place in the middle of the nineteenth century. It is illustrated by Winterhalter's painting of the Empress Eugénie and her ladies, sitting in a glade, a beauty spot. There is not a man about. There is not a gallant to gather flowers, to sit on the grass with the eight court ladies who are as beautiful as Eugénie. The gentlemen refused to come. They didn't want to recline on the hard earth and eat cold food.

But that was nearly a hundred years ago. And men

as is well known have become enfeebled over the years. They do not say it audibly but now when they take their marriage vows they know that they do faithfully promise to love, honor, and go on picnics.

My father's attitude was a little different. He didn't not like picnics, but he didn't like them either. Yet he wasn't neutral. He simply had a pessimistic approach to the whole idea. He saw we enjoyed them and he liked doing things in a family group, but he preferred to have the group center at home, which would be more comfortable.

"You stay at home," said my mother, "and have a chop."

This wasn't what my father wanted at all. He never wanted to be alone. He wanted people around him in his own dining room.

"Besides," said my mother, "it will clear out the house."

My father had no patience with this argument either. He never saw any need for clearing out anything.

"And," said my mother, "it will be a beautiful afternoon."

The word had not then been invented but my father now began to use a form of sabotage. And the sabotage consisted in a strange, an almost diabolic power which he possessed — a power over nature. He stepped out on the lawn, looked over the lake, and sniffed the west breeze.

"The wind is wrong," he announced. As he said this the leaves quivered and the lake rippled a little in the other direction.

"Nonsense," said my mother. "There is blue sky everywhere."

In answer to my father's glance a small white cloud appeared on the horizon.

"Take several flashlights; it may be hard to find our way home through the storm."

"If it storms," replied my mother, "which it won't, it will be an adventure."

My father also had no sympathy with my mother's craving for adventure, which in his eyes involved only the unexpected and a miscarriage of plans. But he too had taken his faithful vows. He knew that come a blizzard, the picnic would take place.

"What time do we start?" he asked.

"Oh, around four," said my mother.

"At four?"

"Around four," repeated my mother. She had learned of old not to commit herself too exactly on the time. Once announced it would become to my father an irrevocable engagement like a public performance which must take place on schedule. My father was a professional and distrusted the amateur quality that is the essence of a picnic.

We were to go by carriage, by foot, and by water. Alice had recently come under the spell of the works of Maurice Hewlett, particularly a volume called *The Forest Lovers*, and had christened her canoe after the lean tanned Hewlett hero, Bill Senhouse. Her brush had slipped in painting the name on the canoe's prow and it had come out *Bill Henhouse*. *Bill Henhouse* was the only canoe which owned a back rest and it was to support my father.

At ten minutes to four he stepped out on the lawn and gave the Siegfried whistle. This is the call that Siegfried blows on his horn when he challenges the dragon to combat. My father always used it. He did not blow it as an assembly to arms, nor yet as a cry for help. It was a sort of summons, which meant "Everyone come to me immediately and do my bidding. Carry things."

I had heard him use it for so many years that I thought he had invented it. The first time I heard Siegfried intone it in the forest I instinctively stiffened to attention, got ready to move, and then wondered how on earth Siegfried had gotten hold of that call of my father's.

My father used it mostly in railway stations for it was a convenient way to gather his family about him. Once in Milan when we were getting ready to take a train, my father blew and a musical Italian answered the call and then went on with the variations. We scattered in two directions and were overcome with embarrassment when we rounded up with the wrong Siegfried, who in turn, pleasantly surprised that one whistle could bring three excited young girls carrying Baedekers, blew again to see what else might appear. My father answered him, thinking one of us was asking for a clearer direction as to his position. An interested little group formed which grew larger as the calls mounted in crescendo, for the Italian knew his Wagner and was quite ready to go through the second act.

Two of us became very agitated over this to us mortifying confusion and tried to shut the Italian up by screaming at him excitedly, "*Mio padre!*"

The onlookers became even more interested and the Italian, thinking I suppose that this was some new kind of foreign blackmail involving paternity, suddenly looked at us with no pleasure at all, and, abruptly ceasing his rendition of Siegfried, left us rapidly. My father's only feeling was one of indignation that a stranger had tried to take over a hunting horn which didn't belong to him at all and had poached on his and Valhalla's territory.

Today the whistle meant, "If we don't start we will be late."

"Late for what!" shouted my mother.

"And," the whistle continued, "everyone help me find my Spanish cape."

This was a long, dark brown cloak with chains across the neck which my father had bought in Barcelona, and which had the remarkable quality of fitting every occasion. It was good to sit on, for charades, it looked in a weird way appropriate when slung over a tuxedo, and it made an excellent pillow. My father loved this cape. He really could not go off on any expedition without it. We found it and after two more whistles we assembled.

A great argument now ensued as to which dogs should not go. We knew that they all would go but old feeble Rama, so we tried to ease my father into *Bill Henhouse* quickly and get him started before he became too specific in his desires. My father was like the thin red line that holds the pass against overwhelming odds and never knows when it is beaten.

"One of them will meet a porcupine," he warned as he sank down against the back rest.

He folded the Spanish cape carefully at his feet and Alice struck out with her paddle. On land Alice moved in a Hewlett reverie, but on the water she went into a *Last of Mohicans* frenzy and the canoe shot out over the lake. My father lay back and looked about. He loved the beauty of a late afternoon and never lost his pleasure in watching light and shadow. His voice came to us clearly and happily. He had relaxed and we on shore relaxed in relief with him.

And then we all saw it. In the water a gray head was following. Rama, ancient and shaky, who never went out from the shore over his knees, was swimming after the canoe. He was making the great gesture. Nothing would keep him back today. We all shouted at once. My father's repose suddenly left him.

"What has happened!" he called agitatedly and tried to stand up.

One and all, our only fear was for Rama. None of us were concerned that the canoe might tip, that my father might land under it. What child, if given the choice between dog or father, hesitates?

The Mohican turned the canoe and somehow Rama was hauled on board. We saw him dripping on the Spanish cloak with his head on my father's knee. What a happy omen for the evening that he would be with us. We watched my father wrap the cape more tightly about him and then put on his own sweater. The afternoon had suddenly grown cooler.

If nine people go on a picnic there are nine violent and divergent opinions expressed as to the best place to eat. If fifteen people go, there are fifteen contrary con-

victions. It is as though a decision were being made as
to where the cornerstone should be laid for the found-
ing of the city of Athens. It is the same with the building
of a fire. There are nine or fifteen views from individuals
who all claim to be experts and who all have passionately divergent feelings concerning the logs on top, the
kindling on top, cooking in the flames, cooking on
coals. No majority view is even reached as to which direction the wind is coming from.

My father was moved twice and protested once more,
but amiably, when a rug was spread out again and he
was assured that if he would just sit here he would be
wonderfully comfortable.

"I tell you all if you will move to that knoll we will
be protected from the wind which is off shore and we
will all have something soft to sit on."

"But you're on moss," I told him. I had picked the
spot myself.

Again my father exhibited his spooklike power. He
rose, pulled up the rug and — two sharp rocks had appeared. They had not been there before; my father had
conjured them up.

"Now don't let's hurry," said Aunt H. "This is the
lovely hour of the day."

"Not eat!" cried Anita.

Anita was the youngest. Like a Balkan country which

has no power in its own right, she achieved her ends by demanding from larger nations more than she thought she could get, and accepting the compromise which was usually better than she had hoped for. She made shifting alliances but generally preferred to fight her own battles and achieve her ends by being vociferous and by being noticed.

"Look at that pink cloud," said my aunt.

"Couldn't I have one piece of chocolate cake?" begged Anita. "I'm starving." This was the familiar Balkan cry.

"They're turning gray in the west," said my father.

"You've got a lot of extra plums," said Anita. "I peeked."

"It looks like a snowy Vesuvius," marveled Aunt H.

We all sat back and gazed at the rosy sunset. The fire had been started, Rama occupied three quarters of my father's rug, Punk lay again across Walker's chest; Rosamond and Polly, stretched out by each other, were comparing the muscles of their arms. All was quiet.

"Quit it, Anita!" said Blair.

Anita was putting little pebbles inside his sneakers.

Aunt H. looked contentedly at the group, which had relaxed. This was the way she liked it.

"I double-dare anyone to climb that biggest cliff

backwards without touching his hands once!" cried Alice, springing up.

My aunt shuddered. Just when calm had finally been achieved, when all disputes had at last been settled, Alice, in my aunt's eyes, invariably thought up some feat of strength which involved motion and danger.

"Oh Alice!" she groaned.

Everyone was on his feet. Alice turned to me.

"As poor little Gretchen thinks she gets dizzy" — Alice's voice lingered over the word "thinks" — "she can use one hand."

I seethed over this. I knew if I attempted the cliff, sportsmanship would now demand that I did not use any support.

"I've got to help unpack the sandwiches," I said piously.

There were knowing croaks from my sisters and they all departed. I watched their figures as they spread out over the cliff. Then with one of those rapid and remarkable *volte-face* of the imagination, I saw myself leading them, both hands over my head, the highest of all — how daring! Suddenly my foot slipped and I hurtled to the ground — dead. Then they'd be sorry. I sat there happily contemplating their grief.

My parents and my aunt now began one of those conversations which were so odd. They started a form of reminiscence which seemed to give them incredible pleasure and yet to my ears was quite incomprehensible.

"H.," said my mother, "do you remember that time in Augusta when Orville Baker — "

"I always thought he was quite right," said my aunt.

"And yet," said my father, "the whole thing could have been handled differently."

Then they all laughed.

"And do you remember," remembered my father, "that day in Washington when Mrs. Blaine — "

"She just didn't see why you wanted to bring him, Walter," said my mother.

None of their stories were real stories. They never had a proper beginning, a middle, and an end. Why did it please them so to recall to each other those odd fragments which they all knew anyhow and yet were so frustratingly inclusive to a listener? What was there to recommend being grown-up? I got out the bacon. Maybe I could have the fun of cooking it myself without interference.

We sat in a circle by the fire eating. Walker and Blair between them were dividing a cake called White Mountain. Well, that was fair. They were leaving tomorrow.

Again came that awful reminder. I put it out of my mind with another hard-boiled egg.

"Are you finished with that chop?" asked Polly, eyeing my father.

"Why?"

"Because I want to give the bone to Rama."

"I am going to eat the marrow," said my father, defiantly clinging to the chop.

"Poor Rama is so hungry," Polly persisted.

Seven chops lay between Rama's paws.

"Quit it, Anita!" said Walker. Anita was squeezing a tomato over the cake's frosting.

"Let's all play a game," suggested my mother.

"What game?" I asked.

This question of mine was to get proof positive that by no possible stretch of the imagination would the game prove to be a thin concealment for teaching us something. All of us with the solidarity of a trade-union resisted learning except when it was unavoidable, and we were adept at spotting those sneaky tricks of parents whereby they introduce the spelling of long words, or the naming of the capitals of states, under the guise of fun.

"I love my love with an A," began my aunt, "because he is amiable. I hate him because he is arrogant."

My father took P. "I love her because she is philanthropic. I hate her because she is phlegmatic." He went on with her attributes. "She lives in Philadelphia and her name is Philomel."

Polly's turn came.

"I love my love with a W because he is a werewolf. I hate him because he is a wicious Wagnerite. He eats *Wurst*, he drinks wegetable soup, he wears wormy woolen wests, and his name is Walter."

Alice's eyes gleamed. "Doesn't he also have wilted woile wristlets over his wrinkled warts?" she asked.

"Full of wermin," added Polly.

My father sighed deeply and looked at his watch. As is described in a military communiqué, a situation deteriorated rapidly under our hands. We liked, we preferred, pushing things too far.

"I think — " began Aunt H.

"And," said Blair, "this wampire worships wirgins."

We looked at Blair admiringly. This was getting good.

"A walet-de-chambre wrecked his wedlock," I added, eager to show my speed.

" — that we had better gather up the paper," continued my aunt.

"But a Wenetian Wenus," contributed Rosamond.

"Wox Pop cries enough!" exclaimed my father.

"Quit it, Anita!" cried Walker and Blair simulta-

and he started to shake. But it was not the tremor of old age, it was the quiver of excitement. He was saying: —

"Get up, you fools! Go crazy with me. It's autumn, here at last. This is a night for hunting!"

"Rama!" we exulted.

The wind mounted and the storm grew wilder as the leaves blew down in streams about us. We smelled the damp earth, we held up our faces to the rain, and all at once we were drunk with a zany happiness. We sang, we shouted, reckless at last with a sense of power. A bad night? — This was a night to be alive.

neously. Anita was running toward the lake with their jackets. They rose in pursuit. Horrible screams now came from the shore to which no one paid any attention. Ten minutes later Anita reappeared. There was tar on her dress and gravel in her hair, but her face was radiant. At last she had reached her objective — she had received attention.

> By the light, by the light, by the light
> Of the silvery moon — the silvery moon.[1]

We sang it together.

And then the rain began to fall.

"It's just a shower," said my mother.

"It's the equinoctials," said my father.

"We have lost the top to the thermos," said my aunt.

"Let's all go swimming!" said Alice.

The rain increased and small whitecaps appeared on the lake.

"I am going back in *Bill Henhouse*," said my mother, "and you are going in the buggy, Walter."

"Of course I'm going back in *Bill Henhouse*," declared my father, "I swim better than you."

"You do not," said my mother, "you don't swim well at all!"

---

[1] Copyright 1909, Jerome H. Remick Co. Copyright renewed and assigned to Remick Music Corp. Used by permission.

A violent discussion began between my parents as to their relative merits. Then, as is the strange way of argument, they arrived, by stages entirely logical to themselves, at a passionate dispute concerning the new wallpaper for the living room.

"I want French gray," cried my mother.

"No! No!" shouted my father. "The old-gold sample is the right one!"

The rain poured over them.

"Put on your sweater, Anita!" exclaimed my mother suddenly.

"I'm boiling," answered Anita.

"It's going to be quite a storm," said Aunt H. "I'm starting. You'd better come soon, boys." Her canoe disappeared with Punk standing in the prow.

Then suddenly we realized that Rama was not with us. We called, we shouted, but he had disappeared.

"Rama! Rama!" I screamed, suddenly filled with panic.

My father stood gloomily waiting under a pine, wrapped in his Spanish cloak.

"During my life," he announced, "I have been on some five hundred picnics and always a dog vanishes and never in my experience has a dog been lost."

"But this is Rama!" I cried. Had he fallen in the lake and, feebly struggling to climb up some embankment,

drowned? Frantically we ran up the shore. Twice we heard the Siegfried whistle and withstood its command. The third time, like an old captivity, it drew us back.

My mother and father had settled their disagreement that the canoe was safe for neither of them by both of them climbing into it together.

"It's getting dark," called my father over the water. "It's a bad night. You must start home."

We did not trouble to answer this meaningless request. Walker set his watch. We would wait a half hour and then search through the backwoods. We huddled together in a damp group under two trees, and we were silent. Each of us was lost in his own thoughts which were stretching out again toward that dreaded place called the Future.

"What a way for summer to end," and I was filled with a dreadful sadness. Where was the grand climax, the bang for the send-off which the glow of the morning had promised? I remembered once more what I had sworn if anything happened to Rama. I would shrivel like Dorian Gray.

"Time's up," said Walker, and then he gave a cry. Galloping toward us through the mist was a huge gray figure. It came tearing over the rocks and a big wet paw was laid on my shoulder. It was Rama, his hair matted with mud and twigs. There was a savage look in his eye

Acknowledgments

The author wishes to extend especial thanks to Mr. Irving Berlin for his kind permission to reprint "When the Midnight Choo-Choo Leaves for Alabam'."

Grateful acknowledgment is made to The Macmillan Company for permission to quote a passage from *The Great Divide* by William Vaughn Moody; to Houghton Mifflin Company for permission to include a selection from Margaret Sidney's *Five Little Peppers Grown Up*; to Music Publishers Holding Corporation for permission to print a verse from the song "Moon Dear," and a quotation from the song "By the Light of the Silvery Moon."